15—

DR. RAY M. FRANK

Children of the Days

Children of the Days

A Calendar of Human History

Eduardo Galeano

Translated by Mark Fried

NATION
BOOKS
New York

Published by Nation Books,
A Member of the Perseus Books Group
116 East 16th Street, 8th Floor
New York, New York 10003

Nation Books is a co-publishing venture of the Nation Institute and the Perseus Books Group

Books published by Nation Books are available at special discounts for bulk purchases in the United States by corporations, institutions, and other organizations. For more information, please contact the Special Markets Department at the Perseus Books Group, 2300 Chestnut Street, Suite 200, Philadelphia, PA 19103, or call (800) 810-4145, ext. 5000, or e-mail special.markets@perseusbooks.com.

Cataloguing-in-Publication data for this book are available from the Library of Congress.

ISBN: 978-1-56858-747-9 (hardcover)
ISBN: 978-1-56858-971-8 (e-book)

10 9 8 7 6 5 4 3 2 1

Acknowledgments

I cannot thank all of the friends who made this book possible or the authors of the many works I consulted. These friends and authors would not fill a stadium, but almost.

However, I can dedicate the end result to those who had the patience to read and comment on the early drafts, which yearned to be final drafts and turned out to be almost final, because there was always something to correct or change, to take out or put in: Ramón Akal, Mark Fried, Karl Hübener, Carlos Machado and Héctor Velarde.

This book is for Helena Villagra. No words needed.

—*In Montevideo, at the end of the year 2011*

And the days began to walk.
And they, the days, made us.
And thus we were born,
the children of the days,
the discoverers,
life's searchers.

—GENESIS, according to the Mayas

JANUARY

January 1

TODAY

Today is not the first day of the year for the Mayas, the Jews, the Arabs, the Chinese or many other inhabitants of this world.

The date was chosen by Rome, imperial Rome, and blessed by Vatican Rome, and it would be an overstatement to say that all humanity celebrates today as the crossing from one year to the next.

That said, today we ought to acknowledge that time treats us rather kindly. Time allows us, its fleeting passengers, to believe that this day could be the very first day, and it gives us leave to want today to be as bright and joyous as the colors of an outdoor market.

January 2

From Fire to Fire

On this day in 1492 Granada fell, and with it fell Muslim Spain.

Triumph of the Holy Inquisition: Granada was the last Spanish kingdom where mosques, churches and synagogues could live side by side in peace.

That same year the conquest of America began, when America was still a mystery without a name.

And in the years that followed, in distant bonfires, the same flames would consume the books of Muslims, of Jews and of America's indigenous peoples.

Fire was the only fate for words born in hell.

January 3

Memory on Legs

On the third day of the year 47 BC, the most renowned library of antiquity burned to the ground.

After Roman legions invaded Egypt, during one of the battles waged by Julius Caesar against the brother of Cleopatra, fire devoured most of the thousands upon thousands of papyrus scrolls in the Library of Alexandria.

A pair of millennia later, after American legions invaded Iraq, during George W. Bush's crusade against an imaginary enemy, most of the thousands upon thousands of books in the Library of Baghdad were reduced to ashes.

Throughout the history of humanity, only one refuge kept books safe from war and conflagration: the walking library, an idea that occurred to the grand vizier of Persia, Abdul Kassem Ismael, at the end of the tenth century.

This prudent and tireless traveler kept his library with him. One hundred and seventeen thousand books aboard four hundred camels formed a caravan a mile long. The camels were also the catalogue: they were arranged according to the titles of the books they carried, a flock for each of the thirty-two letters of the Persian alphabet.

January 4

LAND THAT ATTRACTS

Today in 1643, Isaac Newton was born.

Newton never had any lovers as far as we know, male or female.

Terrified of infections and ghosts, he died a virgin, touched by no one.

But this fearful man had the courage to investigate and reveal the movement of the heavenly bodies,

the composition of light,

the speed of sound,

the conduction of heat

and the law of gravity, the earth's irresistible force of attraction, which calls to us and by calling reminds us of our origin and our destiny.

January 5

Land That Speaks

George Washington Carver dreamed about God.

"Ask of me whatever you wish," God offered.

Carver asked Him to reveal the secrets of peanuts.

"Ask the peanut," God told him.

George, a child of slaves, dedicated his life to resurrecting lands slain by the slave plantations.

In his laboratory, which looked like an alchemist's kitchen, he developed hundreds of products made from peanuts and sweet potatoes: oil, cheese, butter, sauces, mayonnaise, soap, stains, dyes, inks, syrups, glues, talcum . . .

"The plants tell me," he explained. "They'll talk to anyone who knows how to listen."

When he died on this day in 1943 he was nearly eighty years old and still handing out recipes and advice, still teaching in an unusual university, the first in Alabama to accept students who were black.

January 6

LAND THAT AWAITS

In the year 2009, Turkey restored the citizenship denied to Nazim Hikmet and acknowledged at last that its most beloved and derided poet was Turkish.

He could not enjoy the good news: he had died half a century earlier, in the exile that lasted much of his life.

His land awaited him, but his books were outlawed and he was too. The banished poet wished to return:

> I still have things to do.
> I met up with the stars, but I could not count them.
> I drew water from the well, but I could not offer it.

He never returned.

January 7

The Granddaughter

Soledad, granddaughter of Rafael Barrett, liked to recall the words of her grandfather:

"If Good does not exist, we'll have to invent it."

Rafael, Paraguayan by choice, revolutionary by vocation, spent more time in jail than at home, and he died in exile.

The granddaughter was riddled with bullets in Brazil on this day in 1973.

Lance Corporal Anselmo, rebel sailor, revolutionary leader, was the one who turned her in.

Fed up with losing, repenting everything he had dreamed and desired, he named, one after another, all of his comrades in the struggle against the Brazilian military dictatorship and sent them to the torture chamber or the slaughterhouse.

Soledad, his woman, he left for last.

Lance Corporal Anselmo pointed out the place where she was hiding, and then he left.

He was already at the airport when the first shots rang out.

January 8

I Will Not Say Good-bye

In 1872, by order of the president of Ecuador, Manuela León was executed.

The president in his decree called Manuela "Manuel," so there would be no evidence that a gentleman like himself was sending a woman, even a stupid Indian, to the firing squad.

Manuela had stirred up town and country, and caused the Indian masses to rise against forced labor and the payment of tribute. As if that were not enough, she also committed the impertinence of challenging Lieutenant Vallejo, a government official, to fight a duel before the astonished eyes of his soldiers, and in open combat her lance humiliated his sword.

When this, her final day, arrived, Manuela faced the firing squad without a blindfold. Asked if she had anything to say, she answered, in her language:

"*Manapi.*"

Nothing.

January 9

ELEGY TO BREVITY

Today in Philadelphia in 1776, the first edition of *Common Sense* rolled off the press.

Thomas Paine, the author, maintained that independence was only common sense given the humiliation of being a colony and the ludicrous nature of hereditary monarchy, which might as easily crown an ass as a lion.

The 48-page book spread faster than water or wind, and became one of the fathers of US independence.

In 1848, Karl Marx and Friedrich Engels wrote the twenty-three pages of *The Communist Manifesto*, which began by warning, "A specter is haunting Europe . . ." It turned out to be the most influential book of the twentieth century's revolutions.

Twenty-six pages summed up the exhortation to outrage, *Indignez-vous!*, that Stéphane Hessel published in the year 2011. Those few words helped unleash earthquakes of protest in a number of cities. For many days and nights, outraged people in the thousands occupied streets and squares against the global dictatorship of bankers and warmongers.

January 10

Distances

The car coughed and sputtered.

Inside, packed tight and bouncing about, was a band of musicians. They were on their way to enliven a gathering of poor farmers, but for a while now they had been lost on the boiling roads of Argentina's Santiago del Estero.

Bereft of bearings, they had no one to ask. Nobody, not a soul remained in that desert that had once been a forest.

Suddenly, out of a cloud of dust, a girl on a bicycle appeared.

"How much farther?" they asked.

"Less," she said.

And off she went into the dust.

January 11

The Pleasure of Going

Today in 1887 in Salta, the man who was Salta was born: Juan Carlos Dávalos, founder of a dynasty of musicians and poets.

As the tellings tell it, he was the first to drive a Model T, the "Ford with a moustache," in those parts of northern Argentina.

His Model T snorted and smoked as its wheels rolled forward. It moseyed down the road. Turtles stopped to wait for it.

A neighbor came up to him, greeted him with a worried face, commented, "But Mr. Dávalos . . . at this pace, you'll never get there."

The driver responded, "I don't travel to get. I travel to go."

January 12

THE RUSH TO GET THERE

On this morning in the year 2007, a violinist gave a concert in a subway station in Washington, DC.

Leaning against a wall, alongside the usual litter, the musician, who looked more like a local kid, played the works of Schubert and other classics for three-quarters of an hour.

Eleven hundred people hurried by without slowing their pace. Seven paused a bit longer than a moment. No one applauded. Some children wanted to stay, but were dragged off by their mothers.

No one realized he was Joshua Bell, one of the most esteemed virtuosos in the world.

The *Washington Post* had organized the concert. It was their way of asking, "Do you have time for beauty?"

January 13

EARTH THAT BELLOWS

In the year 2010, an earthquake swallowed a large chunk of Haiti and left more than two hundred thousand people dead.

The following day in the United States, a television preacher named Pat Robertson explained what had happened. This shepherd of souls revealed that the blacks of Haiti were to blame, that their freedom was responsible. The Devil had liberated them from French slavery and now he was collecting his due.

January 14

THE HAITIAN CURSE

The earthquake in Haiti was the culminating tragedy of a country without shade, without water, devastated by imperial greed and the war against slavery.

The dethroned slavers explain it another way: Voodoo was and is to blame for all the country's misfortunes. Voodoo doesn't deserve the name religion. It is nothing but African superstition, black magic, a black obsession, the Devil's thing.

The Catholic Church, which has no shortage of faithful believers willing to sell the fingernails of saints or feathers from the wings of the archangel Gabriel, got Haiti to outlaw voodoo in 1845, 1860, 1896, 1915 and 1942.

In recent times, evangelical sects took up the battle against superstition. They come from the country of Pat Robertson, a country that has no thirteenth floor in its skyscrapers, no row thirteen in its airplanes, where civilized Christians who believe God created the world in seven days are in the majority.

January 15

THE SHOE

In 1919 Rosa Luxemburg, the revolutionary, was murdered in Berlin.

Her killers bludgeoned her with rifle blows and tossed her into the waters of a canal.

Along the way, she lost a shoe.

Some hand picked it up, that shoe dropped in the mud.

Rosa longed for a world where justice would not be sacrificed in the name of freedom, nor freedom sacrificed in the name of justice.

Every day, some hand picks up that banner.

Dropped in the mud, like the shoe.

January 16

The Wet Law

On this day in 1920, the Senate of the United States approved the Volstead Act, thus confirming once again that prohibition is the best publicity.

Thanks to the law that declared the country dry, alcohol production and consumption flourished and Al Capone and his men killed and earned more than ever.

In 1933, General Smedley Butler, who had led the US Marines in sixteen medal-winning campaigns on three continents, confessed that what had inspired his men was Al Capone's success in Chicago.

January 17

The Man Who Executed God

In 1918, in the midst of the revolutionary upheaval in Moscow, Anatoly Lunacharsky presided over the court that judged God.

A Bible sat in the chair of the accused.

According to the prosecutor, throughout history God had committed many crimes against humanity. The defense attorney assigned to the case argued that God was not fit to stand trial due to mental illness; but the tribunal sentenced Him to death.

At dawn on this day, five rounds of machine-gun fire were shot at the heavens.

HOLY WATER

In the time of the Holy Inquisition, Spaniards who bathed were suspected of Muslim heresy.

From Mohammed came the adoration of water.

Mohammed was born in the desert back in the year 570, and there, in the kingdom of thirst, he founded the religion of water-seekers.

He said what God, Allah, had told him to say: on the road to salvation, one must pray five times a day, bending down until the chin touches the ground, and before each prayer one must purify oneself with water.

"Cleanliness is half of faith," he said.

January 19

With Him Was Born an Era

In 1736, the Scot James Watt was born.

It is said he did not invent the steam engine, but in his modest workshop he was certainly the one who, without any great expectations, perfected the device that would power the Industrial Revolution.

From that point on, his machine gave rise to other machines that turned peasants into workers, and suddenly, bewilderingly, today became tomorrow and packed yesterday off to prehistory.

January 20

Sacred Serpent

In 1585, at their third episcopal conference, the bishops of Mexico forbade the painting or sculpting of serpents on church walls, retables or altars.

The exterminators of idolatry had by then noticed that those tools of the Devil failed to provoke repulsion or fear among the Indians.

The pagans worshipped snakes. In the Biblical tradition serpents had been scorned ever since that business about Adam's temptation, but America was a loving serpentarium. The sinuous reptile was a sign of good harvests, the lightning bolt that brings on the rains, and every cloud was home to a water snake. A plumed serpent was the god Quetzalcóatl, who had departed on the winding waters.

January 21

They Walked on Water

In the year 1779, English conquistador James Cook witnessed a strange spectacle in the islands of Hawaii.

A pastime as dangerous as it was inexplicable: the natives of Kealakekua Bay loved standing on the waves and riding them.

Was Cook the first spectator of the sport we now call surfing?

Maybe it was more than that. Maybe there was more to the rite of the waves. After all, those primitives believed that water, mother of all life, was sacred, but they did not kneel or bow before their divinity. They walked on the sea in communion with her energy.

Three weeks later, Cook was stabbed to death by the walkers on water. The magnanimous explorer, who had already given Australia to the British Crown, never could make a gift of Hawaii.

January 22

A Kingdom Moves

On this January day in 1808, the exhausted ships that had left Lisbon two months before arrived on the coast of Brazil without bread or water.

Napoleon was trampling the map of Europe and at the Portuguese border he unleashed the stampede: the Portuguese court, obliged to change address, marched off to the tropics.

Queen Maria led the way. Right behind her came the prince and the dukes, counts, viscounts, marquises and barons, all wearing the wigs and sumptuous attire inherited later on by the carnival of Rio de Janeiro. On their heels, butting up against each other in desperation, came priests and military officers, courtesans, dressmakers, doctors, judges, notaries, barbers, scribes, cobblers, gardeners . . .

Queen Maria was not quite in her right mind, which is a nice way to say she was off her rocker, but she pronounced the only reasonable phrase to be heard amid that bunch of lunatics: "Not so fast, it's going to look like we're running away!"

January 23

CIVILIZING MOTHER

In 1901, the day after Queen Victoria breathed her last, a solemn funeral ceremony began in London.

Organizing it was no easy task. A grand farewell was due the queen who gave her name to an epoch and set the standard for female abnegation by wearing black for forty years in memory of her dead husband.

Victoria, symbol of the British Empire, lady and mistress of the nineteenth century, imposed opium on China and virtue on her own country.

In the seat of her empire, works that taught good manners were required reading. Lady Gough's *Book of Etiquette*, published in 1863, established some of the social commandments of the times: one must avoid, for example, the intolerable proximity of male and female authors on library shelves.

Books could only stand together if the authors were married, such as in the case of Robert Browning and Elizabeth Barrett Browning.

January 24

Civilizing Father

On this day in 1965 Winston Churchill passed away.

In 1919, when presiding over the British Air Council, he had offered one of his frequent lessons in the art of war:

"I do not understand this squeamishness about the use of gas . . . I am strongly in favor of using poisoned gas against uncivilized tribes. The moral effect should be so good . . . and would spread a lively terror."

And in 1937, speaking before the Palestine Royal Commission, he offered one of his frequent lessons on the history of humanity:

"I do not admit that a great wrong has been done to the Red Indians of America or the black people of Australia . . . by the fact that a stronger race, a higher-grade race . . . has come in and taken their place."

January 25

The Right to Roguery

The people of Nicaragua celebrate the Güegüense and laugh right along with him.

During these days, the days of his fiesta, the streets become stages where this rogue spins yarns, sings ditties and reels off dance-steps, and by labor and grace of his mummery everyone becomes a storyteller, a singer, a dancer.

The Güegüense is the daddy of Latin American street theater.

Since the beginning of colonial times, he has been teaching the arts of the master trickster: "When you can't beat 'em, tie 'em. When you can't tie 'em, tie 'em up."

Century after century, the Güegüense has never stopped playing the fool. He's the font of fatuous gibberish, the master of devilries envied by the Devil himself, the de-humbler of the humble, a fucking fucked fucker.

January 26

The Second Founding of Bolivia

On this day in the year 2009, a plebiscite said yes to a new constitution proposed by President Evo Morales.

Up to this day, Indians were not the sons and daughters of Bolivia: they were only its hired hands.

In 1825 the first constitution bestowed citizenship on three or four percent of the population. The rest, indigenous people, women, the poor, the illiterate, were not invited to the party.

For many foreign journalists, Bolivia is an ungovernable country, incompetent, incomprehensible, intractable, insane. They've got the wrong "in": they should just admit that for them Bolivia is invisible. And that should come as no surprise, for until today Bolivia was blind to itself.

January 27

Open Your Ears

On this day in 1756, Wolfgang Amadeus Mozart was born. Centuries later, even babies love the music he left us.

It has been proven time and again that newborns cry less and sleep better when they listen to Mozart.

His welcome to the world is the best way of telling them, "This is your new home. And this is how it sounds."

January 28

OPEN YOUR MIND

Long before the printing press, Emperor Charlemagne set up in Aachen large teams of copyists who built the finest library in Europe.

Charlemagne, who did so much for reading, did not know how to read. He died an illiterate, at the beginning of the year 814.

January 29

HUMBLY I SPEAK

Today in 1860 Anton Chekhov was born.
He wrote as if he were saying nothing.
And he said everything.

January 30

The Catapult

In 1933 Adolf Hitler was named Germany's chancellor. Soon after, he presided over an immense rally, as befitted the new lord and master of the nation.

Modestly he screamed: "I am founding the new era of truth! Awaken, Germany! Awaken!" Rockets, fireworks, church bells, chants and cheers echoed his words.

Five years earlier, the Nazi Party had won less than three percent of the vote.

Hitler's Olympic leap to the summit was as spectacular as the simultaneous fall into the abyss of Germany's wages, employment, the mark and you name it.

Germany, crazed by the collapse of everything, unleashed a witch-hunt against the guilty parties: Jews, Reds, homosexuals, Gypsies, the mentally retarded and those afflicted by the habit of thinking too much.

January 31

WE ARE MADE OF WIND

Today in 1908, Atahualpa Yupanqui was born.

In life they were three: guitar, horse and he. Or four, counting the wind.

FEBRUARY

February 1

An Admiral Torn to Pieces

Blas de Lezo was born in Guipúzcoa in 1689.

This admiral of the Spanish Armada defeated English pirates off the Peruvian coast, subjugated the powerful city of Genoa, trounced the city of Oran in Algeria and in Cartagena de Indias, fighting with few ships and a lot of guile, humiliated the British Navy.

In the course of his twenty-two battles, a cannonball took off one of his legs, a piece of shrapnel cost him an eye and a musket ball left him with only one arm.

"Halfman," they called him.

February 2

THE GODDESS IS CELEBRATING

Today on the coasts of the Americas people pay homage to Iemanyá.

On this night the mother goddess of all fish, who came from Africa centuries ago on the slave ships, rises up from the foam of the sea and opens her arms wide. The current brings her combs, brushes, bottles of perfume, cakes, candies and other offerings from sailors dying from love and fear, of her.

Iemanyá's friends and relatives from the African Olympus usually come along to the party:

Xangô, her son, who unleashes the rains from the heavens;

Oxumaré, the rainbow, guardian of fire;

Ogún, blacksmith and warrior, ruffian and womanizer;

Oshún, the lover who sleeps in the rivers and never erases what she writes;

and Exú, who is Satan of hell and also Jesus of Nazareth.

February 3

Carnival Takes Wing

In 1899 the streets of Rio de Janeiro went wild dancing to the song that launched the history of carioca carnival parades.

That luscious pleasure was called "O abre alas"; the dance was a maxixe, Brazil's uproarious answer to those stiff ballroom set pieces.

The songwriter was Chiquinha Gonzaga, a composer since childhood.

At the age of sixteen, her parents married her off, and the Marquis of Caxias was godfather at the wedding.

At twenty, her husband insisted she choose between music and family. "I don't understand life without music," she said, and off she went.

Her father announced that the family's honor had been besmirched and he accused Chiquinha of having inherited her flair for sin from some black grandmother. He declared her dead and forbade anyone in his house from mentioning the name of that loose woman.

February 4

The Threat

Her name was Juana Aguilar, but she was called Juana the Long, for the scandalous size of her clitoris.

The Holy Inquisition received several denunciations of that "criminal excess," and in the year 1803 the Royal Audience of Guatemala sent a surgeon, Narciso Esparragosa, to examine the accused.

This expert in anatomy warned that such a clitoris could be dangerous, as was well known in Egypt and other kingdoms of the Orient, and he found Juana guilty of "flouting the natural order."

February 5

In Two Voices

They grew up together, the guitar and Violeta Parra.

When one called, the other came.

The guitar and she laughed together, cried together, mused together, believed together.

The guitar had a hole in its breast.

So would she.

On this day in 1967, the guitar called and Violeta did not come.

Then or ever again.

THE WAIL

Bob Marley was born poor and slept on the studio floor when he recorded his first songs.

In a few short years he became rich and famous, sleeping on a feather bed, cuddling Miss World, adored far and wide.

But he never forgot that he was more than himself.

Through his voice sang the resonance of times long past, the fiesta and fury of warrior slaves who for two centuries drove their owners crazy in the mountains of Jamaica.

THE EIGHTH BOLT

Roy Sullivan, a Virginia forest warden, was born on this seventh day in 1912, and during his seventy years he survived seven lightning bolts:

In 1942 lightning tore off a toenail.

In 1969 another bolt singed off his eyebrows and eyelashes.

In 1970 a third charred his left shoulder.

In 1972 a bolt left him bald.

In 1973 another burned his legs.

In 1976 a bolt gashed one ankle.

In 1977 a seventh bolt seared his chest and belly.

But the bolt of lightning that split his skull in 1983 did not come from the heavens.

They say it issued from a woman. A word she said, or didn't.

They say.

February 8

General Smooch

In 1980 an extraordinary demonstration hit the streets of the Brazilian city of Sorocaba.

Under the military dictatorship, a court had outlawed kisses that undermined public morals. The ruling by Judge Manuel Moralles, which punished such kisses with jail terms, described them this way:

> Some kisses are libidinous and therefore obscene, like a kiss on the neck, on the private parts, etc., and like the cinematographic kiss in which the labial mucosa come together in an unsophismable expansion of sensuality.

The city responded by becoming one huge kissodrome. Never had people kissed so much. Prohibition sparked desire and many were those who out of simple curiosity wanted a taste of the *unsophismable* kiss.

February 9

Marble That Breathes

Aphrodite was the first female nude in the history of Greek sculpture.

Praxiteles carved her wearing nothing except a tunic fallen about her feet, and the city of Cos insisted that he clothe her. But another city, Cnidus, offered her a temple. There the most womanly of goddesses, the most goddessly of women, took up residence.

Although she was enclosed and well guarded, people were wild about her and flocked to see her.

On a day like today, fed up with the harassment, Aphrodite fled.

February 10

A VICTORY FOR CIVILIZATION

It happened north of the Uruguay River. The king of Spain bestowed upon his father-in-law, the king of Portugal, seven missions of Jesuit priests. The gift included the thirty thousand Guaraní Indians who lived there.

The Guaranís refused to submit and the Jesuits, accused of conspiring with them, were sent back to Europe.

On this day in 1756, in the hills of Caiboaté, the resistance was defeated.

Victory went to the combined armies of Spain and Portugal, more than four thousand soldiers accompanied by horses, cannon and a large number of land grabbers and slave hunters.

Final score, according to the official statistics:

Indians killed, 1,723.

Spaniards killed, 3.

Portuguese killed, 1.

February 11

No

While the year 1962 was being born, an unknown musical group, two guitars, bass, and drums, auditioned for a record company in London.

The boys returned to Liverpool and sat down to wait.

They counted the hours, they counted the days.

When they had no nails left to bite, on a day like today, they received a response. Decca Recording Company told them frankly, "We don't like your sound."

They went further. "Guitar groups are on the way out."

The Beatles did not commit suicide.

February 12

WORLD BREASTFEEDING DAY

Under the sagging roof of the Chengdu station in Sichuan, hundreds of young Chinese women smile for the camera.

All wear new aprons.

All are freshly washed, combed, groomed.

All have just given birth.

They are waiting for the train that will take them to Beijing.

In Beijing they will breastfeed the babies of others.

These milk cows will be well paid and well fed.

Meanwhile, very far from Beijing, in the villages of Sichuan, their own babies will be fed powdered milk.

They all say they do it for their babies, to pay for their education.

February 13

THE DANGER OF PLAYING

In the year 2008, Miguel López Rocha, who was fooling around on the outskirts of the Mexican city of Guadalajara, slipped and fell into the Santiago River.

Miguel was eight years old.

He did not drown.

He was poisoned.

The river contained arsenic, sulfuric acid, mercury, chromium, lead and furans, dumped into its waters by Aventis, Bayer, Nestlé, IBM, DuPont, Xerox, United Plastics, Celanese, and other companies from countries that prohibit such largesse.

February 14

STOLEN CHILDREN

The sons and daughters of the enemy were war booty during the Argentine military dictatorship, which not so long ago stole more than five hundred children.

But many more, over a much longer period, were stolen by Australia's democracy, with consent from the law and applause from the public.

In the year 2008, Australian Prime Minister Kevin Rudd apologized to the aboriginal communities that had been stripped of their sons and daughters for more than a century.

State agencies and Christian churches had kidnapped the children and placed them with white families to save them from poverty and crime, and to civilize them and distance them from savage customs.

"To whiten the race," people used to say.

February 15

More Stolen Children

"Marxism is the worst form of mental illness," ruled Colonel Antonio Vallejo Nájera, psychiatrist supreme in Generalissimo Francisco Franco's Spain.

He had studied Republican mothers in prison and proven that they harbored "criminal tendencies."

To defend the purity of the Iberian race, threatened by Marxist degeneration and maternal delinquency, thousands of newborns and infants, children of Republican parents, were kidnapped and plopped into the arms of families devoted to the cross and sword.

Who were those children? Who are they, so many years later?

No one knows.

Franco's dictatorship falsified the records to cover its tracks and ordered everyone to forget: it stole the children and it stole their memory.

February 16

The Condor Plan

Macarena Gelman was one of the many victims of Operation Condor, the common market of terror that linked South America's dictatorships.

Macarena's mother was pregnant with her when the Argentine generals sent her to Uruguay. The Uruguayan dictatorship oversaw the birth, killed the mother and handed the newborn daughter to a police chief.

Throughout her childhood Macarena was tormented by the same inexplicable nightmare: she was being chased by several men armed to the teeth, and night after night she would wake up crying.

The nightmare stopped being a mystery when Macarena discovered the true story of her life. That was when she realized she had been dreaming her mother's real panic: while Macarena was taking shape in the womb, her mother was fleeing the military witch hunt that caught up with her in the end and sent her to her death.

February 17

The Celebration That Was Not

The peons on the farms of Argentina's Patagonia went out on strike against stunted wages and overgrown workdays, and the army took charge of restoring order.

Executions are grueling. On this night in 1922, soldiers exhausted from so much killing went to the bordello at the port of San Julián for their well-deserved reward.

But the five women who worked there closed the door in their faces and chased them away, screaming, "You murderers! Murderers, get out of here!"

Osvaldo Bayer recorded their names. They were Consuelo García, Ángela Fortunato, Amalia Rodríguez, María Juliache and Maud Foster.

The whores. The virtuous.

February 18

BEREFT OF HIM

When Michelangelo learned of the death of Francesco, who was his apprentice and much more, he took a hammer and smashed the marble he was sculpting.

A short while later, he wrote that such a death:

> . . . had been God's will, but it caused me grave harm and infinite pain. The saving grace lies in the fact that Francesco, who in life kept me alive, by dying taught me to die without sorrow. I had him for twenty-six years . . . Now only infinite misery remains. Most of me went with him.

Michelangelo lies buried in Florence, in the church of Santa Croce.

He and his inseparable Francesco used to sit on the steps of the church to enjoy, in the vast plaza below, the duels fought with kicks and blasts of the ball that we now call soccer.

February 19

Perhaps This Is How Horacio Quiroga
Would Have Written About His Own Death

Today I died.

In the year 1937 I learned that I had a cancer that was untreatable.

I knew that death, after me always, had caught up with me.

I confronted death, face to face, and I told him: "This war is over."

I said: "You win."

I said: "But when is my choice."

And before death killed me, I killed myself.

February 20

At the end of the nineteenth century, Juan Pío Acosta lived near Uruguay's border with Brazil.

In those lonely parts, his work kept him on the road, moving from town to town.

He traveled by stagecoach, along with eight other passengers in first, second and third class.

Juan Pío always bought a third-class ticket, which was the least expensive.

He never understood why there were different prices. Everyone had the same seats, whether they paid more or paid less: jammed in, eating dust, jolted relentlessly.

He never understood why until one bad winter day, when the wagon got stuck in the mud. The coachman ordered:

"First-class, stay where you are!"

"Second-class, get off!"

"And those in third . . . start pushing!"

February 21

The World Shrinks

Today is International Mother Language Day.

Every two weeks, a language dies.

The world is diminished when it loses its human sayings, just as when it loses its diversity of plants and beasts.

In 1974 Angela Loij died. She was one of the last Ona Indians from Tierra del Fuego, way out there at the edge of the world. She was the last one who spoke their language.

Angela sang to herself, for no one else, in that language no longer recalled by anyone but her:

> *I'm walking in the steps*
> *of those who have gone.*
> *Lost, am I.*

In times gone by, the Onas worshipped several gods. Their supreme god was named Pemaulk.

Pemaulk meant "word."

SILENCE

In Istanbul, known in those days as Constantinople, Paul the Silentiary finished his fifteen love poems in the year 563.

The Greek poet owed his name to his work. He was in charge of silence in the palace of Emperor Justinian.

In his own bed, too.

One of his poems says:

> *Your breasts against my breast,*
> *your lips on my lips.*
> *Silence is the rest:*
> *Tongues that never pause I detest.*

February 23

THE BOOK OF MARVELS

One day like this in 1455, Europe's first book printed with moveable type came off the press and it was a Bible.

The Chinese had been printing books for two centuries, but today Johannes Gutenberg initiated the mass circulation of the most gripping novel in literature.

Novels tell but don't explain, and there is no reason why they should. The Bible does not say what Noah ate to reach the age of seven hundred by the time of the Flood, nor what method Abraham's wife used to become pregnant at ninety, nor does it clarify whether Balaam's ass, when arguing with its owner, spoke in Hebrew.

February 24

A Lesson in Realism

In 1815 Napoleon Bonaparte escaped from his prison on the island of Elba and set off to regain the French throne.

On he marched, accompanied by a steadily growing army, while his former official organ, *Le Moniteur Universel*, swore that the people of France were eager to die to protect King Louis XVIII. The paper said Napoleon had "sullied and raped the soil of the fatherland," called him "foreign outlaw, usurper, traitor, plague, bandit chief, enemy of France who dares befoul the land from which he was expelled," and announced: "This will be his final act of insanity."

In the end the king fled, no one died for him, and Napoleon took his seat on the throne without firing a shot.

The same daily went on to report:

The happy news of Napoleon's arrival in the capital has caused a sudden and unanimous outburst of joy, everyone is hugging, cheers for the Emperor fill the air, in every eye are tears of bliss, all rejoice at the return of France's hero and swear the deepest obedience to His Majesty the Emperor.

February 25

Night of the Kuna

The Panamanian government passed a law commanding "the settlement into civilized life of all existing barbarous, semi-barbarous and savage tribes in the country."

Its spokesman announced: "The Kuna Indians will never again paint their noses, only their cheeks, and they will no longer put rings in their noses, only in their ears. And they will no longer dress in molas, rather in civilized attire."

The religious ceremonies of Kuna women and men, which offended God, were outlawed, as was their mania for governing themselves in their own traditional way.

In 1925, on the night of the twenty-fifth day of the month of the iguana, the Kunas used their knives on all the policemen who forbade them from living their lives.

Ever since, Kuna women wear rings in their painted noses and dress in their molas, a splendid art form done by needle and thread instead of paintbrushes. And Kuna women and men continue holding their ceremonies and assemblies on the two thousand islands where they defend, by hook or by crook, their shared kingdom.

February 26

My Africa

At the end of the nineteenth century, the European colonial powers met in Berlin to divvy up Africa.

Long and hard was the fight over colonial booty, the jungles, rivers, mountains, lands, subsoil, until new borders were drawn, and on this day in 1885 a General Act was signed "in the Name of God Almighty."

The European lords had the good taste not to mention gold, diamonds, ivory, oil, rubber, tin, cacao, coffee or palm oil.

They outlawed calling slavery by its name.

They referred to the companies that provided human flesh to the world market as "charitable institutions."

They cautioned that they acted out of a desire to "regulate the conditions most favorable to the development of trade and civilization."

And if there were any doubt, they clarified that they were concerned with "furthering the moral and material wellbeing of the native populations."

Thus Europe drew a new map for Africa.

Not a single African was present at that summit, not even as decoration.

February 27

Even Banks Are Mortal

"All greenness shall perish," prophesied the Bible.

In 1995 Barings Bank, the oldest in England, faced bankruptcy. A week later it was sold for the sum total of one (1) pound sterling.

The bank had been the financier of the British Empire.

Independence and the foreign debt were born as twins in Latin America. All of us were born owing. In our corner of the world, Barings Bank purchased nations, rented founding fathers, financed wars.

And believed itself immortal.

February 28

WHEN

When he was descending a spiral staircase onboard ship, it occurred to him that protein molecules might travel the same way, in a spiral over a wavy base. The thought turned out to be a scientific breakthrough.

When he discovered that automobiles were the reason he coughed so much in the city of Los Angeles, he invented the electric car, which was a commercial failure.

When he came down with kidney disease and medicine did not help, he prescribed himself healthy food and bombardments of vitamin C. He got better.

When the bombs exploded over Hiroshima and Nagasaki, he was invited to speak at a scientific conference in Hollywood. And when he discovered that he had not said what he wanted to say, he went on to lead the global campaign against nuclear weapons.

When he received the Nobel Prize for the second time, *Life* magazine decried it as an insult to all Americans. By then the government of the United States, suspecting him of communist sympathies, had taken away his passport twice, or perhaps it was because he said that God was an unnecessary idea.

His name was Linus Pauling. He was born along with the twentieth century.

February 29

NOT GONE WITH THE WIND

Today's day tends to drop off the calendar, but every four years it finds its way back.

It is the strangest day of the year.

But there was nothing strange about this day in Hollywood in 1940.

In routine fashion, on February 29 Hollywood gave nearly all of its awards, eight Oscars, to *Gone with the Wind*, which was a long sigh of nostalgia for the good old days of slavery.

Thus Hollywood confirmed its ways. Twenty-five years earlier, its first blockbuster was *Birth of a Nation*, an anthem of praise to the Ku Klux Klan.

MARCH

March 1

Eliza Lynch was digging the grave. With her fingernails.

Slack-jawed, the victorious soldiers let her.

Her pawing raised clouds of red dust and shook the loose strands of red hair spilling across her face.

Francisco Solano López, the country's president, lay at her side.

This woman, now mutilated, did not cry for him, did not even look at him. She threw dirt on him, useless handfuls wanting to bury him in this land that had been his land.

He was gone and Paraguay was gone.

Murdered, the only Latin American country that refused to bow down to the bankers and the merchants.

Five years the war had lasted.

And while Eliza continued hurling fistfuls of earth on the man who had been her man, the sun went down and with the sun went this cursed day in the year 1870.

From the foliage on Cerro Corá, a few birds bid it good-bye.

March 2

WHISTLING, I SPEAK

Whistling is the language of La Gomera.

And since 1999 the tongue preserved by this whistling people has been taught in the schools of the Canary Islands.

In ancient times, the shepherds of La Gomera learned to whistle to communicate from distant hilltops across gorges that multiplied the echoes. Their whistles related news of comings and goings, dangers and delights, work to be done and the days going by.

Though centuries have passed, on that island human whistles remain the envy of birds, as powerful as the voices of the wind and the sea.

March 3

THE FOUNDING MOTHERS OF BRAZIL

This day in 1770 brought an end to the queendom of Teresa de Benguela in Quariterê.

It was one of many sanctuaries of freedom for fugitive slaves in Brazil. For twenty years Teresa had thwarted the soldiers of Mato Grosso's governor. They never did capture her alive.

In these densely wooded hiding places, women did much more than cook and give birth; a number of them were fighters and leaders, like Zacimba Gambá in Espírito Santo, Mariana Crioula in the hinterlands of Rio de Janeiro, Zeferina in Bahia and Felipa Maria Aranha in Tocantins.

In Pará, on the banks of the Trombetas River, no one questioned orders given by Mãe Domingas.

In the vast refuge of Palmares in Alagoas, the African princess Aqualtune governed a free town until it was torched by colonial troops in 1677.

In Pernambuco the community founded in 1802 by two fugitive black sisters, Francisca and Mendecha Ferreira, still exists. It is called Conceição das Crioulas.

Whenever the slavers' troops drew near, the former slave women filled their frizzy African tresses with seeds. As elsewhere in the Americas, they turned their heads into granaries, in case they had to flee at a moment's notice.

March 4

The Saudi Miracle

In 1938 a big story broke: Standard Oil Company had found a sea of oil under the immense sands of Saudi Arabia.

Today that country is the world's top producer of high-profile terrorists and of human rights violations. But the Western powers that so often invoke the Arab threat when they want to sow panic or justify dropping bombs get along famously with this kingdom of five thousand princes. Could it be because Saudi Arabia sells the most oil and buys the most weapons?

March 5

DIVORCE AS GOOD HYGIENE

In 1953 a Luis Buñuel movie called *Él* opened in Mexico.

Buñuel, a Spanish exile, had filmed the novel of another Spanish exile, Mercedes Pinto, which told of the misery of married life.

It ran for a full three weeks on the marquee. Audiences laughed like it was a Cantinflas comedy.

The author of the novel had been booted out of Spain in 1923. She had committed the sacrilege of giving a talk at the University of Madrid with a title that made her intolerable: "Divorce as Good Hygiene."

The dictator, Miguel Primo de Rivera, had her hauled in. He spoke in the name of the Holy Mother Catholic Church, and in a few words he said it all: "Shut up or leave."

Mercedes Pinto left.

From that point on her creative stride, which awakened the earth wherever she tread, left footprints in Uruguay, Bolivia, Argentina, Cuba, Mexico . . .

March 6

THE FLORIST

Georgia O'Keeffe lived and painted for nearly a century and died still painting.

She raised a garden of paintings in the solitude of the desert.

Georgia's flowers—clitoris, vulva, vagina, nipple, belly button—were chalices for a thanksgiving mass for the joy of having been born a woman.

March 7

The Witches

In the year 1770, the English Parliament debated a law to punish wily women.

Perfidious females had been seducing His Majesty's subjects and tricking them into matrimony using such evil arts as "scents, paints, cosmetic washes, artificial teeth, false hair, Spanish wool, iron stays, hoops, high-heeled shoes or bolstered hips."

The authors of these frauds, the bill said, "shall incur the penalty of the law in force against witchcraft and the like misdemeanours and the marriage, upon conviction, shall stand null and void."

Given the technological backwardness of the times, the bill failed to mention silicone, liposuction, Botox, plastic surgery and other medical and chemical innovations.

March 8

Today is International Women's Day.

Over the millennia, thinkers human and divine, all of them male, have taken up the woman question:

Regarding their anatomy:

Aristotle: "Woman is an incomplete man."

Saint Thomas Aquinas: "Woman is the misbegotten product of some defect in the male seed."

Martin Luther: "Men have broad shoulders and narrow hips, and accordingly they possess intelligence. Women have narrow shoulders and wide hips, to keep house and bear and raise children."

Regarding their nature:

Francisco de Quevedo: "Hens lay eggs and women lay men."

Saint John of Damascus: "Woman is a sicked she-ass."

Arthur Schopenhauer: "Woman is an animal with long hair and short sight."

Regarding their fate:

Jehovah said to women, according to the Bible: "Thy husband shall rule over thee."

Allah said to Mohammed, according to the Koran: "Righteous women are obedient."

March 9

The Day Mexico Invaded the United States

On this early morning in 1916, Pancho Villa crossed the border with his horsemen, set fire to the city of Columbus, killed several soldiers, nabbed a few horses and guns, and the following day was back in Mexico to tell the tale.

This lightning incursion is the only invasion the United States has suffered since its wars to break free from England.

In contrast, the United States has invaded practically every country in the entire world.

Since 1947 its Department of War has been called the Department of Defense, and its war budget the defense budget.

The names are an enigma as indecipherable as the Holy Trinity.

March 10

THE DEVIL PLAYED THE VIOLIN

On this night in 1712, the Devil visited the young violinist Giuseppe Tartini and played for him in his dreams.

Giuseppe wanted the music to go on forever, but when he awoke it was gone.

In search of that lost music, Tartini composed two hundred and nineteen sonatas, which he played with fruitless mastery throughout his life.

The public applauded his failures.

March 11

The Left Is the University of the Right

In 1931 a baby named Rupert was born in Australia.

In a few short years Rupert Murdoch became lord and master of the media throughout the world.

His astonishing success came not only thanks to his astute command of the dirty deal. Rupert understood the inner workings of capitalism, secrets he learned as a twenty-something student, when he was an admirer of Lenin and a reader of Marx.

March 12

SLEEP KNOWS MORE THAN WAKEFULNESS

Mount Fuji, symbol of Japan, glows red.

The clouds filling the sky are red with plutonium, yellow with strontium, purple with cesium, all of them bearing cancer and other monstrosities.

Six nuclear plants have exploded.

People flee in desperation but there is nowhere to go. "They tricked us! They lied to us!"

Some throw themselves into the sea or the void, just to hurry fate along.

Akira Kurosawa dreamed this nightmare and filmed it twenty years before the apocalyptic nuclear catastrophe his country suffered at the beginning of 2011.

March 13

A Clear Conscience

On this day in the year 2007, the banana company Chiquita Brands, successor to United Fruit, admitted to financing Colombian paramilitary gangs during seven years, and agreed to pay a fine.

The gangs offered protection against strikes and other untoward behavior by labor unions. One hundred and seventy-three union activists were murdered in the banana region during those years.

The fine was twenty-five million dollars. Not a single penny reached the families of the victims.

March 14

In 1883 a crowd gathered for Karl Marx's funeral in a London cemetery—a crowd of eleven, counting the undertaker.

The most famous of his sayings became his epitaph: "The philosophers have only interpreted the world, in various ways; the point, however, is to change it."

This prophet of global change spent his life fleeing the police and his creditors.

Regarding his masterwork, he said: "No one ever wrote so much about money while having so little. *Capital* will not even pay for the cigars I smoked writing it."

March 15

Voices in the Night

At dawn today in the year 44 BC, Calpurnia woke up in tears.

She had dreamed her husband had been stabbed and was dying in her arms.

Calpurnia told him the dream, and still sobbing pleaded with him to remain at home, for outside only his grave awaited.

The supreme ruler, dictator for life, divine warrior, undefeated god, could not pay heed to a woman's dream.

Julius Caesar pushed her aside and walked toward the Roman Senate, to his death.

March 16

STORYTELLERS

Around this day and others, festivals are held to celebrate people who tell tales out loud, writing in the air.

Storytellers have several divinities to inspire and support them.

One is Rafuema, the grandfather who recounted the origin of the Huitoto people in the Araracuara region of Colombia.

Rafuema told the story that the Huitotos were born from the words that told the story of their birth. And every time he told it, the Huitotos were born again.

March 17

They Knew How to Listen

Carlos and Gudrun Lenkersdorf were born and raised in Germany.

In the year 1973, these two illustrious professors arrived in Mexico. They entered the world of the Mayas in a Tojolabal community and they introduced themselves by saying, "We have come to learn."

The Indians remained silent.

After a while, one of them explained the silence: "This is the first time anyone has told us that."

And there they remained, Gudrun and Carlos, learning year after year.

From the Mayan language they learned that no hierarchy separates subject from object, because I drink the water that drinks me and I am watched by all that I watch. And they learned to greet people in the Maya way:

"I'm another you."

"You're another me."

March 18

WITH THEIR GODS INSIDE

In the Andes, the Spanish conquistadors banished the indigenous gods and stamped out all idolatry.

But somewhere around the year 1560, the gods returned. They traveled on their long wings from who knows where, and they entered the bodies of their children from Ayacucho to Oruro, and inside those bodies they began to dance. The dances, which spelled rebellion, were punished with lash or noose, but the gods kept dancing on and on, announcing the end of all humiliation.

In the Quechua language the word *ñaupa* means "was," but it also means "will be."

March 19

BIRTH OF THE MOVIES

In 1895 the Lumière brothers, Louis and Auguste, shot a very short film of workers leaving a factory in Lyon.

That movie, the first in history, was seen by a small circle of friends and no one else.

Not until December 28 did the Lumière brothers give it a public showing, along with nine more of their shorts, which also recorded fleeting moments from real life.

In the basement of the Grand Café in Paris, that marvelous spectacle, child of the magic lantern, the wheel of life and other arts of illusionists, had its premiere.

Full house. Thirty-five people at a franc a seat.

Georges Méliès was in the audience. He wanted to buy their movie camera. Since they wouldn't sell it to him, he had to invent his own.

March 20

The World Upside Down

On March 20 in the year 2003, Iraq's air force bombed the United States.

On the heels of the bombs, Iraqi troops invaded US soil.

There was collateral damage. Many civilians, most of them women and children, were killed or maimed. No one knows how many, because tradition dictates tabulating the losses suffered by invading troops and prohibits counting victims among the invaded population.

The war was inevitable. The security of Iraq and of all humanity was threatened by the weapons of mass destruction stockpiled in United States arsenals.

There was no basis, however, to the insidious rumors suggesting that Iraq intended to keep all the oil in Alaska.

March 21

The World as It Is

In the entire history of human butchery, World War II was the war that killed the most people. But the accounting came up short.

Many soldiers from the colonies never appeared on the lists of the dead. They were Australian aborigines, Indians, Birmanians, Filipinos, Algerians, Senegalese, Vietnamese, and so many other black, brown and yellow people obliged to die for the flags of their masters.

When they are alive, people are ranked first, second, third or fourth class. When they are dead too.

March 22

We are made of water.

From water life bloomed. Rivers of water are the blood that nourishes the earth, and of water too are the cells that do our thinking, the tears that do our crying and the recollections that form our memory.

Memory tells us that today's deserts were yesterday's forests and that the dry world knew well enough to stay wet in those remote days when water and earth belonged to no one and to everyone.

Who took the water? The monkey that raised the club. If I remember correctly, that's how the movie *2001: A Space Odyssey* begins. The unarmed monkey, meanwhile, got clubbed to death.

Sometime later, in the year 2009, a space probe discovered water on the moon. The news sparked plans of conquest.

Sorry, moon.

March 23

Why We Massacred the Indians

With a well-aimed swipe, General Efraín Ríos Montt overthrew another general in the year 1982 and proclaimed himself president of Guatemala.

A year and a half later, the president, a pastor of the California-based Church of the Word, claimed victory in the holy war that exterminated four hundred and forty indigenous communities.

He said the feat would not have been possible without the assistance of the Holy Spirit, who commanded his intelligence services. Another important collaborator, his spiritual advisor Francisco Bianchi, explained to a correspondent of the *New York Times*:

"The guerrillas have many collaborators among the Indians. Those Indians are subversives, aren't they? And how do you put an end to subversion? Obviously, you have to kill those Indians. And then people will say, 'You are massacring innocents.' But they are not innocent."

March 24

Why We Disappeared the Disappeared

On this day in the year 1976, the military dictatorship that would disappear thousands of Argentines was born.

Twenty years later, General Jorge Rafael Videla explained to a journalist, Guido Braslavsky:

"No, they could not be shot. Let's pick a number, say five thousand. Argentine society would not have put up with so many executions, two yesterday in Buenos Aires, six today in Córdoba, four tomorrow in Rosario, and on and on until we reached five thousand . . . No, that would not have worked. Should we reveal where the remains lie? But in the sea, in the River Plate, in the Riachuelo, what could we possibly show? At one point, consideration was given to making the list public. But then we realized that as soon as they are declared dead there will be questions to which we cannot reply: who killed them, when, where, how . . ."

March 25

The Annunciation

On a day like today, more or less, the archangel Gabriel came down from heaven and the Virgin Mary learned that the child of God was living in her womb.

Relics of the Virgin are now worshipped in churches all over the world:

the shoes and slippers she wore,

her nightgowns and her dresses,

hairnets, diadems, combs,

veils and locks of hair,

traces of the milk that Jesus sucked

and her four wedding rings, even though she married only once.

March 26

Maya Liberators

On this night in 1936, Felipa Poot, a Maya Indian, was stoned to death in the town of Kinchil.

Dying with her under the hail of stones were three other women, also Mayas, who had fought at her side against sadness and fear.

They were killed by "the divine caste," which is what those who owned the land and people of the Yucatán called themselves.

March 27

In the year 2010, the public relations firm Murray Hill Inc. told the politicians who claim to govern to stop play-acting.

A short while before, the United States Supreme Court had removed all limits on corporate donations to electoral campaigns; for a much longer while, the bribes legislators received from lobbyists had been legal.

Applying the same logic, Murray Hill Inc. launched its own candidacy for US Congress in the state of Maryland. It was high time to do away with intermediaries:

"This is our democracy. We bought it. We paid for it. Now it's time we got behind the wheel ourselves. Vote Murray Hill Incorporated for the best democracy money can buy."

Many people thought this was a joke.

March 28

Manufacturing Africa

When it opened in 1932, *Tarzan of the Apes* drew long lines at the movie houses.

Tarzan's howl from Hollywood has been the language of Africa everywhere ever since, even though the actor, Johnny Weissmuller, was born in Romania and never set foot in Africa.

Tarzan's vocabulary had its limits. He only knew how to say, "Me Tarzan, you Jane," but he swam like no one else, winning five gold medals at the Olympics, and he yelled like no one had ever yelled.

That king-of-the-jungle howl was the work of Douglas Shearer, a soundman who mixed voices for gorillas, hyenas, camels, violins, sopranos and tenors.

Female fans besieged Johnny to the end of his days, begging him to howl.

March 29

The Jungle Was Here

Miracle in the Amazon: in the year 1967 a huge gusher of oil erupted in Lago Agrio.

From that moment, and for a quarter of a century, Texaco Petroleum Company sat at the table, napkin at throat, knife and fork in hand, stuffing itself with oil and gas, and shitting eighteen billion gallons of poison on the Ecuadorian jungle.

The Indians had never heard the word "pollution." They learned its meaning when fish went belly up in the rivers, lakes turned to brine, trees withered on the banks, animals fled, nothing grew in the soil and people were born sick.

Several presidents of Ecuador, all of them above suspicion, collaborated in this undertaking, which earned a chorus of selfless applause from the publicists who praised it, the journalists who celebrated it, the lawyers who defended it, the experts who justified it and the scientists who absolved it.

March 30

Maruja had no idea how old she was.

Of her years before, she said nothing. Of her years after, she expected nothing.

She was neither pretty nor ugly nor indifferent.

She walked with a shuffle, a duster, a broom or a spoon in her fist.

Awake, she buried her head below her shoulders.

Asleep, she buried her head between her knees.

When she spoke, she kept her eyes on the ground, as if she were counting ants.

She had worked in the homes of others for as long as she could remember.

She had never been outside the city of Lima.

Many times she changed houses and she felt at home in none.

At last she found a place where she was treated as a person.

Within a few days, she left.

She was starting to like it.

March 31

Today in 1631 John Donne died in London.

This contemporary of Shakespeare's published almost nothing during his lifetime.

Centuries later, we are lucky to have a few of the verses he left behind.

Like this:

> *Twice or thrice had I loved thee,*
> *Before I knew thy face or name . . .*

Or this:

> *It sucked me first, and now sucks thee,*
> *And in this flea, our two bloods mingled be . . .*
> *This flea is you and I, and this*
> *Our marriage bed, and marriage temple is . . .*

APRIL

April 1

THE FIRST BISHOP

In 1553 the first bishop of Brazil, Pedro Fernandes Sardinha, set foot on these shores.

Three years later, south of Alagoas, the Caeté Indians ate him for lunch.

Some Brazilians are of the opinion that the meal was an invention of the colonial power, a pretext to steal the Caetés' land and exterminate them in a prolonged "holy war."

Other Brazilians believe the story occurred more or less as told, that Bishop Sardinha, who carried his fate in his fishy name, was the involuntary founder of the national cuisine.

April 2

Manufacturing Public Opinion

In 1917 President Woodrow Wilson announced that the United States would enter World War I.

Four and a half years earlier, Wilson had been elected as the peace candidate.

Public opinion embraced with the same enthusiasm his pacifist speeches and his declaration of war.

Edward Bernays was the principal author of this miracle.

When the war was over, Bernays acknowledged that he had used doctored photographs and made-up anecdotes to spark pro-war sentiment.

This public relations success kicked off a brilliant career.

Bernays went on to advise several presidents and the world's most powerful businessmen.

Reality is not what it is; it's what I tell you it is. We can thank him, more than anyone else, for the modern techniques of mass manipulation that can convince people to buy anything from a brand of soap to a war.

April 3

Good Guys

In 1882 a bullet pierced the neck of Jesse James. It was shot by his best friend, to collect the reward.

Before becoming the country's most famous outlaw, Jesse had fought against President Lincoln for the pro-slavery army of the South. When his side lost, he had to change jobs, and Jesse James's gang was born.

The gang started by pulling off what some say was the very first train robbery in the history of the United States. Wearing their Ku Klux Klan masks, they fleeced every passenger. Then they turned their hand to holding up banks and stagecoaches.

Legend has it that Jesse was something like a Robin Hood of the Wild West, who stole from the rich and gave to the poor, only no one ever met a poor person who received a coin from his hands.

Yet there is no question about his generosity to Hollywood. The movie industry can thank him for forty films, nearly all of them successes, in which stars from Tyrone Power to Brad Pitt have gripped his smoking revolver.

April 4

The Ghost

In 1846 Isidore Ducasse was born.

It was wartime in Montevideo and he was baptized by cannon fire.

As soon as he could, he went off to Paris, where he became the Comte de Lautréamont and his nightmares helped give rise to surrealism.

He only dropped into the world for a visit. During his brief life he set fire to language, burned brightly through his words and disappeared in a puff of smoke.

April 5

DAY OF LIGHT

It happened in Africa, in Ife, the sacred city of the Yoruba kingdom, maybe on a day like today or who knows when.

An old man, very ill, brought his three sons before him and announced: "My most cherished things will belong to the one who can fill this room completely."

And he sat outside to wait while night fell.

One of his sons brought all the straw he could find, but it filled the room only halfway.

Another brought all the sand he could carry, but again half the room was left empty.

The third lit a candle.

And the room was filled.

April 6

Night Crossing

In certain towns lost in the mountains of Guatemala, anonymous hands sew tiny worry dolls.

A surefire remedy for anxiety, they calm stormy thoughts and come to the rescue when insomnia threatens.

These minuscule worry dolls don't say a thing. They heal by listening. Huddled under the pillow, they absorb sorrows and regrets, doubts and debts, all the phantoms that undermine a peaceful sleep, and they carry them off, magically far off, to the secret place where night is never an enemy.

April 7

THE DOCTOR'S BILL

Three thousand seven hundred years ago the king of Babylonia, Hammurabi, set down in law the rates dictated by the gods for medical services:

If with his bronze lancet the physician cureth a man of a serious wound or an eye abscess, ten silver shekels shall he receive.

If the patient be a poor man, five silver shekels shall the physician receive.

If the patient be the slave of someone, two silver shekels shall his owner give the physician.

If a physician causeth the death of a free man or the loss of an eye, his hands shall be cut off.

If a physician causeth the death of the slave of a poor man, one of his own slaves shall the physician give him. If a physician causeth the loss of a slave's eye, half the slave's value shall he pay.

April 8

THE MAN WHO WAS BORN MANY TIMES

On this day in 1973, Pablo Diego José Francisco de Paula Juan Nepomuceno María de los Remedios Cipriano de la Santísima Trinidad Ruíz y Picasso, more commonly known as Pablo Picasso, passed away.

He was born in 1881. It seems he liked it, because he kept being born and reborn.

April 9

Good Health

In the year 2011 the population of Iceland said no for the second time to the International Monetary Fund.

The Fund and the European Union had decided that Iceland's three hundred twenty thousand inhabitants should be liable for the bankruptcy of its bankers, for which each and every Icelander owed a foreign debt of twelve thousand euros.

Such socialism in reverse was rejected in two plebiscites. "The debt is not our debt. Why should we pay it?"

In a world unhinged by the financial crisis, this small island lost in the waters of the North Atlantic offered us all a healthy lesson in common sense.

April 10

MANUFACTURING DISEASE

Healthy? Unhealthy? It all depends on your point of view. From the point of view of the pharmaceutical industry, bad health can be very good.

Take shyness, for example. This character trait used to be acceptable, even attractive. That is, until it became an illness. In the year 1980 the American Psychiatric Association decided that shyness was a psychological ailment and included it in its *Manual of Mental Disorders*, which is periodically updated by the high priests of Science.

Like all illnesses, shyness requires medication. Ever since the news broke, Big Pharma has made a fortune selling hope to patients plagued by this "social phobia," "allergy to people," "severe medical problem" . . .

April 11

On this day in the year 2002, a coup d'état turned the president of a business association into the president of Venezuela.

His glory did not last long. A couple of days later, Venezuelans filling the streets reinstated the president they had elected with their votes.

Venezuela's biggest TV and radio networks celebrated the coup, but somehow failed to cover the massive demonstrations that restored Hugo Chávez to his rightful place.

Unpleasant news is not worth reporting.

April 12

MANUFACTURING THE GUILTY PARTY

On a day like today in the year 33—a day earlier, a day later—Jesus of Nazareth died on the cross.

His judges had found him guilty of "inciting idolatry, blasphemy and abominable superstition."

Not many centuries later, the Indians of the Americas and the heretics of Europe were found guilty of those same crimes—exactly the same ones—and in the name of Jesus of Nazareth they were punished by lash, gallows, or fire.

April 13

WE KNEW NOT HOW TO SEE YOU

In the year 2009, in the atrium of the convent of Maní in the Yucatán, forty-two Franciscan brothers held a ceremony of restitution for injuries caused to indigenous culture.

"We ask forgiveness of the Maya people, for not having understood their worldview, their religion, for denying their divinities, for not having respected their culture, for having imposed over many centuries a religion they did not understand, for having treated as satanic their religious practices, and for having said and written that these were the work of the Devil and that their idols were Satan himself in the flesh."

Four and a half centuries before, in that very place, another Franciscan brother, Diego de Landa, had burned the Mayas' books, and with them eight centuries of collective memory.

April 14

GRAND OR JUST PLAIN BIG?

In the year 1588 Spain's *Invincible Armada*, then the largest fleet in the world, was defeated in a matter of hours.

In the year 1628 Sweden's most powerful warship, the *Vasa*, also known as *Invincible*, sank on its maiden voyage. It never made it out of Stockholm's harbor.

And on the night of this day in 1912, the world's safest and most luxurious ocean liner, humbly named *Titanic*, hit an iceberg and went down. This floating palace had few lifeboats, a uselessly small rudder, watchmen without binoculars and warning bells that were never heard.

April 15

THE BLACK PAINTINGS

In 1828 Francisco de Goya died in exile.

Harassed by the Inquisition, he had fled to France.

On his deathbed, between incomprehensible mutterings, Goya spoke of his beloved home on the outskirts of Madrid, on the banks of the Manzanares River. There, painted on the walls, was the best of his work, his most personal.

After his death the house was sold and resold, paintings and all, until the works were finally removed from the walls and transferred onto canvases. In vain they were put up for sale at the Paris Exposition. No one wanted to see, much less buy, those ferocious prophesies of the century to come, in which grief slaughtered color and horror shamelessly revealed its raw face. The Prado Museum did not wish to buy them either, and at the beginning of 1882 they entered its halls by donation.

The "black paintings" are now among the most visited in the museum.

"I painted them for myself," Goya said.

He did not know that he painted them for us.

April 16

In the year 1881, Antonio Machado y Álvarez completed his anthology of flamenco songs, nine hundred couplets from the Gypsy songbook of Andalusia.

> *In olden days tasteless*
> *were all the waves in the sea,*
> *then she spit, my dark-skinned dearest*
> *which was when they turned salty.*

> *Girls with dark complexion*
> *have a gaze that is so weird,*
> *it kills more in a single hour*
> *than death in an entire year.*

> *The day that you were born*
> *a piece of heaven fell to earth.*
> *Not until you cease to live*
> *will heaven regain its girth.*

He published the book and the critics panned it. Flamenco's *cante jondo* evoked their scorn, because it was the work of Gypsies. But that's precisely why these couplets carry their music with them, in their clapping palms and in their stamping feet.

April 17

CARUSO SANG AND RAN

On this night in 1906, tenor Enrico Caruso sang *Carmen* at the Tivoli Opera House in San Francisco.

The ovation carried him all the way to the door of the Palace Hotel.

The master of bel canto slept poorly. As dawn was about to break, a violent tremor knocked him from his bed.

The earthquake, the worst in California history, killed more than three thousand people and demolished half the city's homes.

Caruso started running and did not stop until he got to Rome.

April 18

Keep an Eye on This Guy

Today in 1955 Albert Einstein died.

For twenty-two years the FBI tapped his telephone, read his mail and went through his garbage.

They spied on Einstein because he was a spy for the Russians. So said his bulky police file. The file also said he had invented a death ray and a robot that could read minds. It said Einstein was a member, collaborator or fellow traveler of thirty-four Communist front organizations between 1937 and 1954, and was honorary chair of three Communist organizations. It concluded: "It seems unlikely that a man of his background could, in such a short time, become a loyal American citizen."

Not even death saved him. They continued spying on him. Not the FBI, but his colleagues, men of science who sliced his brain into two hundred forty pieces and analyzed them to find an explanation for his genius.

They found nothing.

Einstein had already warned, "I have no special gift. I am only passionately curious."

April 19

CHILDREN OF THE CLOUDS

In 1987 the king of Morocco finished building a north–south wall across the Sahara Desert, on lands that do not belong to him.

This is the longest wall in the world, exceeded only by the Great Wall of China. All along it Moroccan soldiers block the Saharawi people from entering their land.

Several times the United Nations confirmed the people of Western Sahara's right to self-determination and called for a plebiscite to allow them to determine their own fate.

But the kingdom of Morocco has refused and continues to refuse. That refusal is a confession. By denying the vote, Morocco confesses to having stolen a country.

For forty years the Saharawi people have been waiting. They are condemned to a life sentence of anguish and nostalgia without parole.

They call themselves "children of the clouds," because since time immemorial they have pursued the rains. They also pursue justice, which is harder to find than water in the desert.

April 20

Manufacturing Mistakes

It was among the largest military expeditions ever launched in the history of the Caribbean. And it was the greatest blunder.

The dispossessed and evicted owners of Cuba declared from Miami that they were ready to die fighting for devolution, against revolution.

The US government believed them, and their intelligence services once again proved themselves unworthy of the name.

On April 20, 1961, three days after disembarking at the Bay of Pigs, armed to the teeth and backed by warships and planes, these courageous heroes surrendered.

April 21

The Indignant One

It happened in Spain in a town of La Rioja on the evening of this day in 2011, during an Easter procession.

A huge crowd watched in silence as Jesus Christ, being whipped by Roman soldiers, passed by.

A voice broke the silence.

Seated on his father's shoulders, Marcos Rabasco shouted at the man being whipped: "Fight back! Fight back!"

Marcos was two years, four months and twenty-one days old.

April 22

Einstein once said, "If the bee disappears from the surface of the earth, man would have no more than four years to live. No more bees, no more pollination . . . no more men!"

He said it to a few friends.

The friends laughed.

He did not.

Now it turns out there are fewer and fewer bees in the world.

Today, on Earth Day, let us acknowledge that this is not happening due to God's will or the Devil's curse, but rather because of:

the murder of natural forests and the proliferation of farmed ones;

monocropping for export, which limits plant diversity;

poisons that kill pests and with them everything else;

chemical fertilizers that fertilize money and sterilize the soil;

and radiation from the machines people buy because advertising tells us to.

April 23

FAME IS BALONEY

Today, World Book Day, it wouldn't hurt to recall that the history of literature is an unceasing paradox.

What is the most popular scene in the Bible? Adam and Eve biting the apple. It's not there.

Plato never wrote his most famous line: "Only the dead have seen the end of war."

Don Quijote de la Mancha never said: "Let the dogs bark, Sancho. It's a sign we are on track."

Voltaire's best-known line was not said or written by him: "I do not agree with what you have to say, but I will defend to the death your right to say it."

Georg Wilhelm Friedrich Hegel never wrote: "All theory is gray, my friend, but green is the tree of life."

Sherlock Holmes never said: "Elementary, my dear Watson."

In none of his books or pamphlets did Lenin write: "The ends justify the means."

Bertolt Brecht was not the author of his most oft-cited poem: "First they came for the Communists / and I didn't speak out because I wasn't a Communist . . ."

And neither was Jorge Luis Borges the author of his best-known poem: "If I could live my life over / I would try to make more mistakes . . ."

April 24

The Perils of Publishing

In the year 2004, for once the government of Guatemala broke with the tradition of impunity and officially acknowledged that Myrna Mack was killed by order of the country's president.

Myrna had undertaken forbidden research. Despite receiving threats, she had gone deep into the jungles and mountains to find exiles wandering in their own country, the indigenous survivors of the military's massacres. She collected their voices.

In 1989, at a conference of social scientists, an anthropologist from the United States complained about the pressure universities exert to continually produce: "In my country if you don't publish, you perish."

And Myrna replied: "In my country if you publish, you perish."

She published.

She was stabbed to death.

April 25

Don't Save Me, Please

During this week in 1951, Mohammad Mossadegh was elected prime minister of Iran in a landslide.

Mossadegh had promised to take back Iran's oil, which had been given away to the British.

But nationalizing oil could lead to the sort of chaos that helps the Communists. So President Eisenhower gave the order to attack and the United States saved Iran. The coup d'état of 1953 put Mossadegh in prison, sent many of his followers to their graves and gave forty percent of the oil Mossadegh had nationalized to US companies.

The following year, far from Iran, President Eisenhower gave another order to attack and the United States saved Guatemala. A coup d'état toppled the democratically elected government of Jacobo Arbenz because he had expropriated the uncultivated lands of the United Fruit Company. Expropriating land could lead to the sort of chaos that helps the Communists.

Guatemala is still paying for that act of kindness.

April 26

Nothing Happened Here

It occurred in Chernobyl in Ukraine in 1986.

It was the worst nuclear catastrophe the world had ever suffered, but the only ones to learn of the tragedy from the first moment were the birds that fled and the worms that dug themselves into the ground.

The Soviet government ordered silence.

Radioactive rain fell over much of Europe and the government continued denying or refusing to speak.

A quarter of a century later, in Fukushima, several nuclear reactors exploded and the Japanese government also remained silent or denied "alarmist versions."

The veteran British journalist Claud Cockburn was right when he suggested, "Never believe anything until it has been officially denied."

April 27

Life's Twists and Turns

The Conservative Party was in power in Nicaragua on this day in 1837 when women won the right to abortion if their lives were in danger.

One hundred seventy years later, in the very same country, legislators who claimed to be Sandinista revolutionaries outlawed abortion "in any circumstance," and thus condemned poor women to prison or the cemetery.

April 28

This Insecure World

Today, on World Day for Safety and Health at Work, it's worth noting that these days nothing is as insecure as a job. More and more workers awaken each day wondering: "Am I about to become excess baggage? Who is going to hire me?"

Many lose their jobs and on the job many lose their lives: every fifteen seconds a worker dies, murdered by what they call "workplace accidents."

Insecurity is the politicians' preferred topic when they want to unleash the hysteria that wins elections. Danger, danger, they declare, on every corner there's a thief, a rapist, a murderer. But those politicians never decry the dangers of working,

or the dangers of crossing the street, since every twenty-four seconds a pedestrian is killed, murdered by what they call "traffic accidents";

or the dangers of eating, since whoever is safe from hunger may well be poisoned by the chemicals in their food;

or the dangers of breathing, since in cities clean air is like silence, a luxury item;

or the dangers of being born, since every three seconds a child dies before reaching the age of five.

April 29

SHE DOESN'T FORGET

Who knows all the shortcuts through Africa's jungles?

Who knows how to evade the menacing approach of ivory hunters and other wild predators?

Who can read her own tracks and the tracks of all others?

Who preserves the memory of all and sundry?

Who emits signals that humans can neither hear nor decipher?

Signals that frighten or assist or threaten or greet from ten miles distant?

It is she, the elephant elder. The oldest, the wisest. The one who walks at the head of the herd.

April 30

This afternoon in 1977, fourteen mothers of disappeared children met for the first time.

From then on they searched as a group, as a group they knocked on doors that would not open. "All for all," they said.

They said, "All for our children."

Thousands upon thousands of children had been devoured by the Argentine military dictatorship, and more than five hundred children had been kidnapped and given to officers as war booty. The papers, radio, TV breathed not a word of it.

A few months after their first meeting, three of those mothers, Azucena Villaflor, Esther Ballestrino and María Eugenia Ponce, also disappeared, just like their children, and like them they were tortured and murdered.

But by then the Thursday meetings were unstoppable. Their white kerchiefs moved round and round the Plaza de Mayo and around the world.

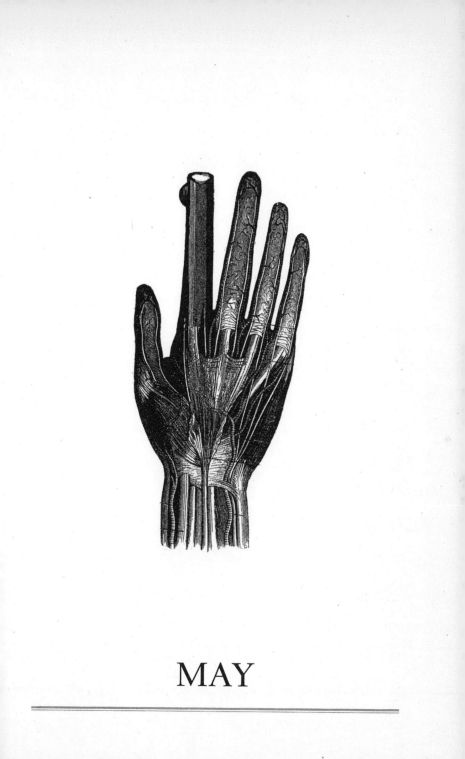

MAY

May 1

The technology of shared flight: the first goose to take off opens the way for the next, who clears the path for the third, and the strength of the third raises the fourth, who then helps the fifth, and the impulse of the fifth pulls along the sixth, who offers wind to the seventh . . .

When the lead goose tires, he goes to the back of the line and leaves his spot to another, who moves to the apex of the V the geese form in the air. Each takes a turn, forward and back, and none of them believes he is supergoose because he flies first or that flying last makes him a loser.

May 2

Operation Geronimo

Geronimo led the Apache resistance in the nineteenth century.

This chief of the invaded earned himself a nasty reputation for driving the invaders crazy with his bravery and brilliance, and in the century that followed he became the baddest bad guy in the West on screen.

Keeping to that tradition, "Operation Geronimo" was the name chosen by the US government for the execution of Osama bin Laden, who was shot and disappeared on this day in 2011.

But what did Geronimo have to do with bin Laden, the delirious caliph cooked up in the image laboratories of the US military? Was Geronimo even remotely like this professional fearmonger who would announce his intention to eat every child raw whenever a US president needed to justify a new war?

The name was not an innocent choice: the US military always considered the Indian warriors who defended their lands and dignity against foreign conquest to be terrorists.

May 3

DISHONOR

At the end of 1979, Soviet troops invaded Afghanistan.

The official justification was to defend a secular government trying to modernize the country.

I was a member of an international tribunal in Stockholm that took up the case in 1981.

I will never forget the dramatic climax of those sessions.

A leading religious figure, representing the Islamic fundamentalists known at that time as "freedom fighters" and now called "terrorists," was giving testimony.

The elderly man screamed, "The Communists have sullied the honor of our daughters! They taught them to read and to write!"

May 4

While the Night Lasts

In 1937 Noel Rosa died at the age of twenty-six.

A musician of the Rio de Janeiro night, who in his short life saw the beach only in photographs, he wrote and sang sambas in the bars of the city that sings them still.

In one of those bars a friend bumped into him at the nocturnal hour of ten in the morning.

Noel was humming a newborn tune.

On the table stood two bottles. One beer, the other cheap rum.

The friend knew that tuberculosis was killing him. Noel saw the worry in his friend's face and felt obliged to instruct him in the nutritive properties of beer. Pointing to the bottle he declared, "This is better for you than a good meal."

The friend, not exactly convinced, pointed at the bottle of rum. "What about that?"

And Noel explained, "How good is a good meal if you don't have something with it?"

May 5

By Singing I Rebuke

In 1932 Noel Rosa recorded his samba "Quem dá mais?," a short history of a country that had been auctioned off:

> *How much will he earn, that auctioneer*
> *who must be Brazilian as well*
> *selling off in lots of three*
> *all of Brazil, pray tell?*

A couple of years later Enrique Santos Discépolo painted a portrait of Argentina's days of infamy in his tango "Cambalache":

> *Today they're all of a piece*
> *the friend, the damned cheat,*
> *the dumbbell, the genius, the thief,*
> *the generous soul, the deadbeat.*
> *Go for it man, get it while you can . . .*

May 6

Apparitions

The stock market crash left journalist Jonathan Tilove without a job.

But in 2009, while cleaning out his office in Washington, he saw the Virgin Mary in a coffee stain on his desk, and his luck changed.

As the crisis deepened and everybody lost faith in economists and politicians and journalists, he wasn't the only one to discover the Virgin in a cheese sandwich or an asparagus plant or a dental X-ray.

May 7

The Party Poopers

In 1954 Vietnamese rebels gave the French army a tremendous beating at their supposedly invulnerable base in Dien Bien Phu. After a century of conquering colonies, glorious France had to exit Vietnam in a hurry.

Then it was the United States' turn. Unbelievable: the greatest power on earth and in space also suffered a humiliating defeat in this tiny, badly armed country populated by the poorest of the poor.

A peasant of slow gait, few words led both of these exploits.

His name was Ho Chi Minh, and they called him Uncle Ho.

Uncle Ho wasn't at all like other revolutionary leaders.

An activist returning from a village once reported that there was no way to organize those people. "They're a bunch of Buddhist yahoos. They spend all day meditating."

"Go back there and meditate," Uncle Ho ordered.

May 8

The Tasmanian Devil

This diabolical monster with flared nostrils and bone-crushing teeth is famous the world over.

But the real devil of Tasmania did not come from hell. It was the British Empire that exterminated the population of this island off Australia, and did so in the noble pursuit of civilizing it.

The last victim of the English war of conquest was named Truganini. A queen dispossessed of her queendom, she died on this day in 1876, and with her died the language and memory of her people.

May 9

Born to Find Him

Howard Carter was born on this morning in 1874, and half a century later he understood why he had come into the world.

The revelation came to him when he discovered the tomb of Tutankhamun.

Carter located it through sheer stubbornness, after years of trying everywhere, battling discouragement and the fearmongering of his fellow Egyptologists.

On the day of the great find, he sat at the foot of the short-lived pharaoh, the boy surrounded by a thousand marvels, and spent long hours in silence.

He returned many times.

One of those times he saw what he had not seen before: there were seeds on the floor.

The seeds had spent three thousand two hundred years waiting for the hand that would plant them.

May 10

The Unforgivable

The poet Roque Dalton wielded a defiant wit, he never learned to shut up or take orders, and he laughed and loved fearlessly.

On the eve of this day in the year 1975, his fellow guerrillas in El Salvador shot him dead while he slept.

Criminals: rebels who kill to punish disagreement are no less criminal than generals who kill to perpetuate injustice.

May 11

MR. EVERYTHING

Eugène François Vidocq died in Paris in 1857.

Beginning the moment he held up his father's bakery at the age of fourteen, Eugène was a thief, a clown, a thug, a deserter, a smuggler, a schoolteacher chasing after little girls, the idol of the bordellos, a businessman, a stool pigeon, a spy, a criminologist, a ballistics expert, the director of the Sûreté Générale (the French FBI), and the founder of the very first private detective agency.

Twenty duels he fought. Five times he turned into a nun or a crippled veteran to escape from jail. He was a master of disguises, a criminal playing a policeman, a policeman playing a criminal, and he was the friend of his enemies and the enemy of his friends.

Sherlock Holmes and other notables of European detective literature owe many of their skills to the tricks Vidocq learned from his life of crime, which he later applied to fighting it.

May 12

LIVING SEISMOGRAPHS

In the year 2008 a terrible earthquake struck China.

The seismograph was invented in China nineteen centuries ago, but no machine warned what was coming.

What raised the alarm were the animals. Scientists paid them no heed, but starting a few days before the catastrophe, hordes of crazed toads took off in every direction, hopping wildly across the streets of Guiyang and other cities, while in the Wuhan zoo tigers roared, peacocks screeched and elephants and zebras threw themselves against the bars of their cages.

May 13

To Sing, to See

To see the worlds of the world, shift your eyes.
To have the birds hear your song, shift your throat.

So say, so know, the ancient sages born at the source of the
Orinoco River.

May 14

Someone Else's Debt

On this day in 1948 the state of Israel was born.

Within a few months, more than eight hundred thousand Palestinians had been deported and more than five hundred of their villages had been turned to rubble.

Those villages, where olive, fig, almond and other fruit trees grew, now lie buried under highways, shopping malls and amusement parks. They are dead and unnamed on the map rechristened by the Government Names Committee.

Not much of Palestine is left. The two thousand years of persecution suffered by the Jewish people was invoked to justify this implacable gluttony, complete with property titles granted by the Bible.

Persecuting Jews had always been a European sport. Now the Palestinians are paying the bill.

May 15

MAY TOMORROW BE MORE THAN
JUST ANOTHER NAME FOR TODAY

In 2011 thousands of homeless and jobless youth occupied the streets and squares of several Spanish cities.

Their outrage spread. Healthy outrage turned out to be more contagious than disease, and the voices of "the indignant" crossed the borders drawn on maps. Their words echoed around the world:

> *They put us in the fucking street and here we are.*
> *Turn off the TV and turn on the street.*
> *They call it a crisis but it's a rip-off.*
> *Not too little money, too many crooks.*
> *Markets rule. I didn't vote for them.*
> *They decide for us without us.*
> *Wage slave for rent.*
> *I'm looking for my rights. Anyone seen them?*
> *If they won't let us dream, we won't let them sleep.*

May 16

OFF TO THE LOONY BIN

Groupers and other fish,
dolphins,
swans, flamingos, albatrosses,
penguins,
buffaloes,
ostriches,
koala bears,
orangutans and other monkeys,
butterflies and other insects
and many more of our relatives in the animal kingdom have homosexual relations, female to female, male to male, for an encounter or a lifetime.

Lucky for them they aren't people or they'd be sent to the loony bin.

Until this day in the year 1990, homosexuality featured on the World Health Organization's list of mental illnesses.

May 17

HOME

The twenty-first century has been walking through time for a few years now, and the number of people without adequate housing has reached one billion.

To solve this problem, experts are looking into the Christian example of Saint Simeon Stylites, who lived for thirty-seven years atop a column.

In the morning Saint Simeon would come down to pray and at night he would tie himself down, so he wouldn't tumble off in his sleep.

May 18

MEMORY'S VOYAGE

In 1781 Túpac Amaru was quartered with an ax in the middle of the Plaza de Armas in Cuzco.

Two centuries later, a tourist asked a barefoot boy who shined shoes in that very spot if he had ever met Túpac Amaru. The little bootblack, without raising his head, said that yes, he knew him. While he continued working, he murmured, practically in secret, "He's the wind."

May 19

THE PROPHET MARK

Mark Twain proclaimed:

"I came in with Halley's Comet in 1835. It is coming again next year and I expect to go out with it ... The Almighty has said, no doubt: 'Now here are these two unaccountable freaks; they came in together, they must go out together.'"

The comet visited the earth around this time in 1910. Twain, impatient, died a month before.

May 20

A RARE ACT OF SANITY

In 1998 France passed a law that reduced the workweek to thirty-five hours.

Work less, live more: Thomas More dreamed of this in *Utopia*, but we had to wait five centuries before a country finally dared commit such an act of common sense.

After all, what are machines for if not to reduce the time we spend working and to lengthen our hours of freedom? Why does technological progress have to come bearing the gifts of anguish and unemployment?

For once, at least, a country dared to challenge all that nonsense.

Sanity did not last. When the thirty-five-hour week was ten years old, it expired.

May 21

In 1906 a pygmy captured in the jungle of the Congo arrived at the Bronx Zoo in New York.

He was named Ota Benga and was exhibited to the public in a cage along with an orangutan and four chimpanzees. The experts explained that this humanoid might represent the missing link, and to confirm their hypothesis they displayed him playing with his hairy brothers.

Sometime later the pygmy was rescued by Christian charity.

They did what they could but it was hopeless. Ota Benga refused to be saved. He would not speak, broke dishes at the table, hit anyone who tried to touch him. He was incapable of working any job, remained silent in the church choir and bit whoever tried to have a picture taken with him.

At the end of the winter of 1916, after ten years of domestication, Ota Benga sat down in front of a fire, took off and burned the clothing he had been obliged to wear, then trained the pistol he had stolen on his heart.

TINTIN AMONG THE SAVAGES

On this day in 1907 Belgian cartoonist Hergé, the father of comic-book hero Tintin, was born.

Tintin incarnated the civilizing virtues of the white race.

In his best-selling adventure, Tintin visited the Congo, still owned by Belgium, and there he laughed heartily at the ridiculous doings of black people and entertained himself hunting.

He shot fifteen antelope, skinned a monkey for a disguise, blew up a rhinoceros with a stick of dynamite and stuck a gun into the open mouths of many crocodiles and pulled the trigger.

Tintin said that elephants spoke much better French than black people. For a souvenir he killed one and pulled out its ivory tusks.

The trip was a lot of fun.

May 23

Manufacturing Power

In 1937 John D. Rockefeller, owner of the world, king of oil, founder of Standard Oil Company, passed away.

He had lived for nearly a century.

The autopsy found not a single scruple.

May 24

THE HERETICS AND THE SAINT

This day in the year 1543 marked the end of Nicolaus Copernicus's life.

He died as the first copies of his book, which demonstrated that the earth moved around the sun, went into circulation.

The Church condemned the book as "false and altogether contrary to Holy Scripture," sent the priest Giordano Bruno to the stake for spreading its ideas, and obliged Galileo Galilei to deny he had read and believed it.

Three and a half centuries later, the Vatican repented of roasting Giordano Bruno alive and announced it would erect a statue of Galileo in its gardens.

God's embassy on earth takes its time to rectify things.

But even as the Vatican pardoned these heresies, it beatified Cardinal Inquisitor Roberto Bellarmino—Saint Robert who art in heaven—the man who charged and sentenced Bruno and Galileo.

May 25

HERESIES

In the year 325 in the city of Nicaea, Emperor Constantine I convened the first ecumenical council of Christendom. During the three months it sat, the three hundred bishops in attendance approved a creed vital for the struggle against heresy, and decided that the word "heresy," from the Greek *hairesis*, which means "choice," from then on would mean "error."

In other words, whoever freely chooses to disobey the owners of the faith is wrong.

May 26

SHERLOCK HOLMES DIED TWICE

The first death of Sherlock Holmes occurred in 1891. His father killed him: the writer Arthur Conan Doyle couldn't stand the fact that his pedantic offspring was more famous than he was. So, up in the Alps he threw Sherlock off a cliff.

The news came out shortly thereafter in *Strand* magazine. Then the whole world dressed in mourning, the magazine lost readers and the writer lost friends.

The resurrection of the most famous of all detectives was not long in coming.

Conan Doyle had no choice but to bring him back to life.

Of Sherlock's second death nothing is known. No one answers the telephone in his Baker Street home. His time must have come by now because we all have to die, though it is curious that his obituary has never appeared in the *Times*.

May 27

Beloved Vagabond

Fernando passed away today in 1963.

He was a free spirit who belonged to everyone and to no one.

When he tired of chasing cats across squares, he'd hit the streets with his singing and guitar-playing buddies and rumba with them from party to party, always chasing the music wherever it happened to be.

He never missed a concert. A critic with a cultivated ear, he'd wag his tail if he liked what he heard, growl if he didn't.

Whenever the dogcatcher got hold of him, a crowd would set him free. Whenever a car nipped him, the best doctors would take him in and treat him.

His carnal sins, committed in the middle of the street, tended to be punished with swift kicks that left him limping, and then the children's brigade of the Progreso Club would give him intensive care.

Three statues of Fernando grace his city, Resistencia, in Argentina's Chaco.

May 28

Today in the year 2006, Pope Benedict, the supreme pontiff of the Roman Catholic Church, took a walk in the gardens of the city called, in Polish, Oświęcim.

At a certain point the scenery changed.

In German the city of Oświęcim is called Auschwitz.

And in Auschwitz, the pope spoke. From the most famous death factory in the world, he asked, "And God, where was He?"

No one told him that God had never changed his address.

He asked, "Why did God remain silent?"

No one pointed out that it was the Church that remained silent, the Church that spoke in God's name.

May 29

Vampires

In the summer of 1725, Petar Blagojevic got out of his coffin in the village of Kisiljevo, bit nine neighbors and drank their blood. By order of the Austrian government, then in charge in these parts, the forces of order killed him definitively by driving a stake through his heart.

Petar was the first officially recognized vampire, and the least famous.

The most successful, Count Dracula, was born from the pen of Bram Stoker in 1897.

More than a century later Dracula retired. What forced him out wasn't the competition from the silly little vampires of Hollywood, which didn't bother him in the least. No, he was tormented by feats of a different magnitude.

Faced with the mighty gluttons who founded banks then made them founder, swilling blood as if the whole world were a neck, he knew his inferiority complex was terminal.

May 30

FROM THE STAKE TO THE ALTAR

On this day in 1431, a nineteen-year-old girl was burned alive in the old marketplace at Rouen.

She climbed the scaffold wearing an enormous cap, which said:

> *Heretic,*
> *Recidivist,*
> *Apostate,*
> *Idolatress.*

After she was burned to death, her body was thrown from a bridge into the Seine, so the waters would carry her far away.

She had been condemned by the Catholic Church and the Kingdom of France.

Her name was Joan of Arc.

Heard of her?

May 31

THE INCOMBUSTIBLE LADY

Signora Girardelli, worker of wonders, left the European public bug-eyed back in the year 1820.

She caressed her arms with lit candles, danced barefoot on red-hot irons, bathed in flames, gulped mouthfuls of boiling oil, swallowed fire, chewed up burning sticks and spit them out as pounds sterling ... After such ardent exhibitions she showed off her unblemished body, her snow-white skin, and basked in applause.

Skeptics said, "These are tricks."

She said not a word.

JUNE

June 1

Saintly Men

In the year 2006 the Charity, Freedom and Diversity Party sought legal recognition in the Netherlands.

This new political group said it represented "men who express their sexuality and erotic lives in free relations with boys and girls."

The party platform called for legalizing child pornography and sexual relations with minors.

Eight years before, these campaigners for charity, freedom and diversity founded International BoyLove Day on the Internet.

The party failed to collect the required number of signatures, never took part in any elections and, in the year 2010, committed suicide.

June 2

INDIANS ARE PERSONS

In 1537 Pope Paul III issued a bull, "Sublimus Dei."

The bull admonished those "who, wishing to fulfill their greed, dare to affirm that Indians should be treated as dumb brutes created for our service, under the pretense that they are incapable of receiving the Catholic Faith."

In defense of the aboriginal people of the New World, it established that "Indians are truly men . . . and thus they may and should, freely and legitimately, enjoy their liberty and the possession of their property, and should not be in any way enslaved."

In America, nobody caught wind of it.

June 3

ATAHUALPA'S REVENGE

The town of Tambogrande slept on a bed of gold.

Gold lay under the houses, unbeknownst to anyone.

The news arrived along with the eviction orders. The Peruvian government had sold the entire town to Manhattan Minerals Corp.

Now you will all be millionaires, they were told. But no one obeyed. On this day in the year 2002, the result of a plebiscite was announced: the inhabitants of Tambogrande had decided to continue living from avocados, mangos, limes and other fruits of the land they had worked so hard to wrest from the desert.

Well they knew that gold curses the places it inhabits: it blows apart the hills with dynamite and poisons the rivers with tailings that contain more cyanide than blessed water.

Maybe they also knew that gold makes people crazy, because with gold the more you eat the hungrier you get.

In 1533, Spanish conquistador Francisco Pizarro ordered Atahualpa strangled, even though the king of Peru had given him all the gold he demanded.

June 4

MEMORY OF THE FUTURE

According to what we learned in school, the discovery of Chile took place in 1536.

The news did not impress the Mapuches, who had discovered Chile three thousand years before.

In 1563 they surrounded the main fort of the Spanish conquistadors.

Besieged by thousands of furious Indians, the fort was on the point of surrender when Captain Lorenzo Bernal clambered up on the palisade and shouted, "We will win in the end! We don't have Spanish women, so we'll have yours. And with them we'll have children who will be your masters."

The interpreter translated. Colocolo, the Indian leader, listened the way one listens to rain fall.

He did not understand the sad prophecy.

June 5

Nature Is Not Mute

Reality paints still lifes.

Disasters are called natural, as if nature were the executioner and not the victim. Meanwhile the climate goes haywire and we do too.

Today is World Environment Day. A good day to celebrate the new constitution of Ecuador, which in the year 2008, for the first time in the history of the world, recognized nature as a subject with rights.

It seems strange, this notion that nature has rights as if it were a person. But in the United States it seems perfectly normal that big companies have human rights. They do, ever since a Supreme Court decision in 1886.

If nature were a bank, they would have already rescued it.

June 6

The Mountains That Were

Over the past two centuries, four hundred seventy mountains have been decapitated in the Appalachians, the North American range named in memory of the region's native people.

Because they lived on fertile lands the Indians were evicted.

Because they contained coal the mountains were hollowed out.

June 7

The Poet King

Nezahualcóyotl died twenty years before Columbus first set foot on the beaches of America.

He was the king of Texcoco in the vast valley of Mexico.

There, he left us his voice:

> It breaks, even if it be gold,
> it shatters, even if it be jade,
> it rends, even if it be a quetzal's plumage.
> Here no one lives forever.
> Princes too come to die.
> All of us must go on to the region of mystery.
> Could it be we came to the earth in vain?
> At least we leave behind our songs.

June 8

SACRILEGE

In the year 1504, Michelangelo unveiled his masterpiece: David stood tall in the main plaza of the city of Florence.

Insults and stones greeted this utterly naked giant.

Michelangelo was obliged to cover its indecency with a grape leaf, sculpted in bronze.

June 9

Sacrilegious Women

In the year 1901, Elisa Sánchez and Marcela Gracia got married in the church of Saint George in the Galician city of A Coruña.

Elisa and Marcela had loved in secret. To make things proper, complete with ceremony, priest, license and photograph, they had to invent a husband. Elisa became Mario: she cut her hair, dressed in men's clothing, and faked a deep voice.

When the story came out, newspapers all over Spain screamed to high heaven—"this disgusting scandal, this shameless immorality"—and made use of the lamentable occasion to sell papers hand over fist, while the Church, its trust deceived, denounced the sacrilege to the police.

And the chase began.

Elisa and Marcela fled to Portugal.

In Oporto they were caught and imprisoned.

But they escaped. They changed their names and took to the sea.

In the city of Buenos Aires the trail of the fugitives went cold.

June 10

Around this time in the year 2010, debate began in Buenos Aires on a bill to legalize gay marriage.

Its enemies launched "God's war against weddings from Hell," but the bill kept clearing the hurdles in its path and on July 15 Argentina became the first Latin American country to recognize the equality of women and men all across the sexual spectrum.

It was a defeat for the ruling hypocrisy, which expects us to live obeying and to die dissembling, and it was a defeat for the Holy Inquisition, which may change its name but never lacks fuel for the fire.

June 11

The Man Who Sold the Eiffel Tower

Count Victor Lustig, prophet of the Wall Street whiz kids to come, adopted several names and several titles of nobility, resided in several prisons in several countries, and in several languages was able to lie with utter sincerity.

At noon on this day in 1925 the count was reading the newspaper in the lobby of the Hotel de Crillon in Paris, when he was struck by one of those great ideas that could finance his appetites whenever he tired of playing poker.

He sold the Eiffel Tower.

He printed up paper and envelopes with the seal of city hall and an engineer crony helped him write technical reports that proved the tower was falling down due to irreparable errors in its construction.

The count visited potential clients, one by one, and invited them to purchase the thousands upon thousands of tons of steel for a song. Because it involved the most public symbol of the French nation, the deal had to be done in secret. Scandal was to be avoided at all cost. The sales took place in silence and with some urgency, since the tower could have collapsed at any moment.

June 12

The Mystery Explained

In the year 2010 the war against Afghanistan divulged its raison d'être: the Pentagon revealed that the country had mineral resources worth more than a trillion dollars.

The Taliban were not among the resources named.

Rather gold, cobalt, copper, iron and above all lithium, an essential ingredient in cellular telephones and laptop computers.

June 13

COLLATERAL DAMAGE

Around this time in 2010 it came out that more and more US soldiers were committing suicide. It was nearly as common as death in combat.

The Pentagon promised to hire more mental health specialists, already the fastest-growing job classification in the armed forces.

The world is becoming an immense military base, and that base is becoming a mental hospital the size of the world. Inside the nuthouse, which ones are crazy? The soldiers killing themselves or the wars that oblige them to kill?

June 14

FLAG AS DISGUISE

On this day in 1982 the Argentine dictatorship lost the war. Without even so much as a shaving nick, the generals, who had sworn to give their lives to recover the Falkland Islands long ago usurped by the British Empire, tamely surrendered.

Here is the military division of labor: these heroic rapists of handcuffed women, these brave torturers and baby-snatchers and pocketers of everything else they could steal, made patriotic speeches; and young recruits from the poorest provinces marched off to the slaughterhouse of those far-off southern islands, where they died from bullets or the cold.

June 15

A Woman Talks

Several Argentine generals were tried for deeds committed during the military dictatorship.

Silvina Parodi, a student accused of being a rabble-rousing troublemaker, was one of the many prisoners who disappeared forever.

Her best friend Cecilia testified in court on this day in the year 2008. She told of the agony she had suffered at the military base and admitted she had been the one who gave them Silvina's name, when she could no longer stand the daily and nightly torture.

"It was me. I took the executioners to the house where Silvina was. I saw them shove her out the door, hit her with their rifle butts, kick her. I heard her scream."

Outside the courtroom, someone came over and asked her in a low voice, "After all that, how did you manage to go on living?"

And she answered, in a voice even lower, "Who told you I'm alive?"

June 16

I'VE GOT SOMETHING TO TELL YOU

Oscar Liñeira was another of the thousands of young men disappeared in Argentina. In military lingo, he was "transferred."

Piero Di Monte, imprisoned at the same base, heard his last words: "I've got something to tell you. You know something? I've never made love. Now they're going to kill me and I never will."

June 17

TOMASA DIDN'T PAY

In 1782 the Quito municipal court ruled that Tomasa Surita had to pay the taxes on some cloth she had bought in Guayaquil.

Only males were legally authorized to buy or to sell, but she was still liable for the taxes.

"Let them collect it from my husband," Tomasa said. "The law thinks we're idiots. If we women are idiots about getting paid, then we'll be idiots about paying too."

June 18

Susan Didn't Pay Either

The *United States of America v. Susan B. Anthony*, Northern District Court of New York, June 18, 1873.

DISTRICT ATTORNEY RICHARD CROWLEY: On the 5th of November, 1872, Miss Susan B. Anthony voted for a representative in the Congress of the United States. At that time she was a woman. I suppose there will be no question about that. She did not have a right to vote. She is guilty of violating a law.

JUDGE WARD HUNT: The prisoner has been tried according to the established forms of law.

SUSAN B. ANTHONY: Yes, your honor, but by forms of law all made by men, interpreted by men, administered by men, in favor of men, and against women.

JUDGE HUNT: The prisoner will stand up. The sentence of the Court is that you pay a fine of one hundred dollars and the costs of the prosecution.

MISS ANTHONY: I shall never pay a dollar.

June 19

Danger: Bicycles!

"I think bicycling has done more to emancipate women than anything else in the world," said Susan B. Anthony.

Her companion in the struggle, Elizabeth Cady Stanton, said, "Woman is riding to suffrage on a bicycle."

Certain physicians, like Philippe Tissié, warned that the bicycle might provoke abortion and cause sterility, while their colleagues insisted that this indecent apparatus might lead to depravity because it gave women pleasure when they pressed their intimate parts against the seat.

The truth is the bicycle gave women mobility, allowed them to leave the house and enjoy a dangerous taste of freedom. And it was the bicycle that sent the pitiless corset, which impeded pedaling, out of the clothes closet and into the museum.

June 20

That Shortcoming

Her soprano voice lent color to every syllable and won ovations in Rio de Janeiro.

By the end of the eighteenth century, Joaquina Lapinha became the first singer from Brazil to conquer Europe.

Carl Ruders, a Swedish opera fan, heard her in the year 1800 in a theater in Lisbon. Enthused, he praised "her good voice, imposing figure and great dramatic sense."

"Unfortunately, Joaquina has very dark skin," Ruders warned, "but she remedies that shortcoming with cosmetics."

June 21

WE ARE ALL YOU

Today's soccer match in 2001 between Treviso and Genoa was a surprise.

One of Treviso's players, the Nigerian Akeem Omolade, was often greeted in Italy's stadiums with whistles and jeers and racist chants.

But today there was silence. The other ten Treviso players had all painted their faces black.

June 22

The World's Waist

In the year 234 before Christ, a sage named Eratosthenes planted a rod at noon in the city of Alexandria and measured its shadow.

Exactly one year later, at the same time on the same day, he planted the same rod in the city of Aswan and it cast no shadow.

Eratosthenes deduced that the difference between shadow and no shadow proved the world was a sphere not a plate. Then he measured the distance between the two cities in steps, and with that information tried to calculate the size of the world's waist.

He was fifty miles off.

June 23

FIRES

At midnight tonight, big bonfires are lit.

Crowds gather around them.

This night will cleanse houses and souls. Old junk and old desires, things and feelings worn out by time, are tossed into the fire to make room for the new to be born.

From the north this custom spread all over the world. It was always a pagan holiday. Always, until the Roman Catholic Church decided tonight would be Saint John's Eve.

June 24

THE SUN

Today, starting at dawn, the sun festival known as Inti Raymi is celebrated on the steppes and peaks of the Andes.

At the beginning of time, the earth and sky were in darkness. There was only night.

When the first woman and the first man emerged from the waters of Lake Titicaca, the sun was born.

Viracocha, god of gods, invented the sun so that woman and man could enjoy the sight of each other.

June 25

The Moon

Chinese poet Li Po died in the year 762 on a night like this one.

A drowning.

He fell from the boat when he tried to hug the moon reflected in the waters of the Yangtze.

Li Po had sought out the moon on other nights.

> *I drink alone.*
> *No friend is near.*
> *I raise my cup,*
> *toast the moon*
> *and my shadow.*
> *Now we are three.*
> *But the moon does not drink*
> *and my shadow only imitates me.*

June 26

THE KINGDOM OF FEAR

Today is International Day Against Torture.

By tragic irony, the Uruguayan military dictatorship was born the following day in 1973 and soon turned the country into one huge torture chamber.

For obtaining information torture was useless or practically useless, but it was very useful for sowing fear, and fear obliged Uruguayans to live by silence or lies.

While in exile, I received an unsigned letter:

> *Lying sucks, and getting used to lying sucks.*
> *But worse than lying is teaching to lie.*
> *I have three children.*

WE ARE ALL GUILTY

Directorium Inquisitorum, published by the Holy Inquisition in the fourteenth century, set down the rules for torture. The most important was: "The accused who hesitates in his responses shall be tortured."

June 28

Hell

Back in the year 960, Christian missionaries invaded Scandinavia and threatened the Vikings: if you persist in your pagan customs you will end up in hell where eternal fires burn.

The Vikings welcomed the good news. They trembled from cold, not fear.

June 29

The Great Heretofore

Some say it's said that today is Saint Peter's Day, and they say he holds the keys to the gates of heaven.

Who knows for sure.

Well-informed sources report that heaven and hell are just two names for the world each of us carries around inside.

June 30

A Nuisance Is Born

Today in 1819 Juana Manso was baptized in Buenos Aires.

The holy waters were to set her on the path to meekness, but Juana Manso was never meek.

Bucking wind and tide she founded secular schools in Argentina and Uruguay where girls and boys studied together, religion was not a required course and corporal punishment was banned.

She wrote the first textbook on Argentine history plus several other works, among them a novel that derided the hypocrisy of married life.

She founded the first public library in the country's interior.

She got divorced when divorce did not exist.

The Buenos Aires papers took great pleasure in mocking her.

When she died, the Church refused her a tomb.

JULY

July 1

One Terrorist Fewer

In the year 2008, the government of the United States decided to erase Nelson Mandela's name from its list of dangerous terrorists.

The most revered African in the world had featured on that sinister roll for sixty years.

July 2

Olympic Prehistory

During the 1904 Olympic Games in the American city of St. Louis, a series of special competitions took place over the course of what they called "Anthropology Days."

Taking part were Native Americans, Japanese Ainu, African pygmies and other specimens on display in the parallel world's fair.

They were not allowed into the formal athletic competitions, begun six weeks earlier and continuing for another three months, although two Zulus in the Boer War exhibit obtained special dispensation to run the marathon and came in fifth and twelfth.

Fred Lorz, white and male, won that race, which was the most popular event. Shortly thereafter, it came out that he had run half the route in a friend's car.

That was the last piece of Olympic chicanery that did not involve the chemical industry.

From then on, the world of sport went modern.

Athletes no longer compete on their own. They carry whole medicine cabinets inside.

July 3

The Stone in the Hole

Three months had passed since King James II outlawed golf in 1457 and still not a single Scot paid any heed.

In vain, the monarch repeated the order: young men must dedicate their best efforts to the art of archery, essential for national defense, instead of wasting time whacking little balls.

But golf was born in Scotland's green pastures back around the year 1000 by shepherds who eased their boredom knocking stones into rabbit holes, and the tradition remained invincible.

Scotland is home to the two oldest golf courses in the world. They are open to the public and entry is practically free. What a rarity: in most of the world this privatized sport belongs to the few, and golf courses gobble up the land and chug the water that belongs to us all.

July 4

THE SOUTHERN CROSS

On this night in 1799, Alexander von Humboldt and Aimé Bonpland discovered the Southern Cross.

Sailing across the immense ocean, they saw these heretofore unseen stars.

The Southern Cross pointed the way to America.

Humboldt and Bonpland did not come to conquer. They wished not to take but to give. And give they did, these scientist adventurers who helped us to see and know ourselves.

Years later, at the end of their trip deep into the South American heartland, Humboldt returned to Europe.

Aimé, "Don Amado," chose to remain behind in this land that had become his own.

To the end of his days, Don Amado collected and classified thousands of unknown plants. He rediscovered lost medicinal herbs from the indigenous store of knowledge and set up free herbal pharmacies for all. He hoed, planted, harvested; he raised children and chickens. He learned and taught, endured prison and practiced love thy neighbor ("starting with the females," he liked to say).

July 5

THE RIGHT TO LAUGH

According to the Bible, King Solomon of Israel did not have a high opinion of laughter. "It's crazy," he said.

And on happiness: "What good is it?"

According to scripture, Jesus never once laughed.

The right to laugh without sin had to wait until this day in 1182, when a baby named Francis was born in the town of Assisi.

Saint Francis of Assisi was born smiling and years later he instructed his disciples, "Be happy. Avoid sad faces, frowns, scowls . . . "

July 6

Fool Me

Today in 1810 Phineas Barnum was baptized in Connecticut.

The baby grew up to found the most famous circus in the world.

It began as a museum of rarities and monstrosities that drew multitudes:

they bowed before a blind slave woman, 161 years old, who had suckled George Washington;

they kissed the hand of Napoleon Bonaparte, 25 inches tall;

and they confirmed that the Siamese twins Chang and Eng were truly attached and that the circus mermaids had genuine fishtails.

Professional politicians of every epoch envy Barnum more than any other man. He was the undisputed master at putting into practice his great discovery: *People love to be fooled.*

July 7

FRIDAMANIA

In 1954 a Communist demonstration marched through the streets of Mexico City.

Frida Kahlo was there in her wheelchair.

It was the last time she was seen alive.

She died shortly thereafter, without fanfare.

A number of years passed before the huge uproar of Fridamania awakened her.

A just restitution or just business? Did this woman, who hated the pursuit of success and prettiness, deserve this? Did the artist of pitiless self-portraits, complete with unibrow and moustache, and bristling with pins and needles and the scars of thirty-two operations, deserve such treatment?

What if all this were much more than a profit-making manipulation? What if it really were time's homage to a woman who turned her agony into art?

July 8

· LEADER FOR LIFE

In 1994 the immortal one died.

His life ended but he lived on.

According to the constitution of North Korea, written by himself, Kim Il Sung was born on the first day of the New Era of Humanity and he was its Eternal Leader.

The New Era he inaugurated carries on. So does he: Kim Il Sung continues ruling from his statues, which happen to be the country's tallest edifices.

July 9

The Suns the Night Hides

In the year 1909 Vitalino was born in Brazil's Northeast.

And the dry earth, where nothing grows, became wet earth to bring forth its children of clay.

In the beginning these were toys shaped by his hands to keep him company in childhood.

The passing of time turned his toys into small sculptures of tigers and hunters, workers with their hoes digging into the hard earth, desert warriors hoisting their rifles, caravans of refugees fleeing drought, guitar players, dancing girls, lovers, processions, saints ...

Thus Vitalino's magic fingers told the tragedy and the festivity of his people.

July 10

Manufacturing Novels

On this fateful day in 1844, the French were left with nothing to read. The magazine *Le Siècle* published the final installment of the nineteen-chapter adventure novel devoured by all France.

It was over. What now? Without *The Three Musketeers*, in reality four, who would risk his life, day in, day out, for the honor of the queen?

Alexandre Dumas wrote this work and three hundred more at a pace of six thousand words a day. His envious detractors said his feat of literary athleticism was only possible because he tended to put his name on pages stolen from other books or bought from the poorly paid pen-pushers he employed.

His interminable banquets, which swelled his belly and emptied his pockets, may have obliged him to mass-produce works for hire.

The French government, for example, paid him to write the novel *Montevideo or the New Troy*, dedicated to "the heroic defenders" of the port city that Adolphe Thiers called "our colony" and that Dumas had never even heard of. The book raised to epic heights the defense of the port against the men of the land, those shoeless gauchos that Dumas called "savage scourges of Civilization."

July 11

Manufacturing Tears

In 1941 all Brazil wept through the first radio soap opera:

Colgate toothpaste presents . . .
"In Search of Happiness!"

The show had been imported from Cuba and adapted to the local context. The characters had plenty of money, but they were doomed. Anytime happiness was within their grasp, cruel Fate ruined everything. Three years went by like this, episode after episode, and not a fly moved when showtime arrived.

Some villages lost in the hinterland had no radios. But there was always someone willing to ride the few leagues to the next village, listen closely to the episode, commit it to memory and return by gallop. Then the rider would recount what he had heard. An anxious crowd gathered to hear his version, much longer than the original, and to savor the latest misfortune, with that unappeasable pleasure the poor feel when they can pity the rich.

July 12

CONSECRATION OF THE TOP SCORER

In 1949 Giampiero Boniperti was the top scorer of the Italian championship and its brightest star.

According to what people say, he was born backwards, kicking-foot first, and he began his voyage to soccer glory in the crib.

The club Juventus paid him a cow for every goal.

Altri tempi.

July 13

THE GOAL OF THE CENTURY

On this day in the year 2002, organized soccer's top brass announced the result of their global online poll, "Pick the goal of the century."

By a landslide, the winner was Diego Maradona's in the 1986 World Cup, when he danced with the ball glued to his foot and left six Englishmen foundering in his wake.

That was the last image of the world for Manuel Alba Olivares.

He was eleven and at that magical moment his eyes tuned out forever. He kept the goal intact in his memory and he recounts it better than the best commentators.

Ever since, to see soccer and other things not quite so important, Manuel borrows the eyes of his friends.

Thanks to them, this blind Colombian founded the soccer club he leads, became and remains the coach of the team, comments on the matches on his radio program, sings to entertain the audience and, in his free time, he works as a lawyer.

July 14

The Losers' Trunk

Helena Villagra dreamed of an immense trunk.

She opened it with a very old key and out of the trunk spilled failed shots on goal, missed penalties, defeated teams. And the failed shots entered the net, the ball gone awry corrected its flight and the losers celebrated their victory. As long as the ball and the dream kept flying, that backwards match would never end.

July 15

An Exorcism

On this night in 1950, the eve of the World Cup final, Moacir Barbosa slept in the arms of the angels.

He was the most beloved man in all Brazil.

But the following day the finest goalkeeper in the world became a traitor to his country: Barbosa failed to block the Uruguayan goal that snatched the trophy from Brazil's grasp.

Thirteen years later, when Maracanã stadium put in new goalposts, Barbosa took the two posts and the crossbar that had humiliated him. He chopped them up with an ax and burned the pieces until they were nothing but ashes.

The exorcism did not save him from damnation.

July 16

My Dear Enemy

White was Brazil's jersey. But once the 1950 World Cup showed white to be unlucky, it was never white again.

The final match was over, Uruguay was world champion and the fans would not leave. Two hundred thousand Brazilians had turned to stone in Maracanã stadium.

On the field a number of players still wandered about.

The two best crossed paths, Obdulio and Zizinho.

They crossed paths. They eyed each other.

They were very different. Obdulio, the victor, was made of steel. Zizinho, the vanquished, was made of music. But they were also very much alike: both had played nearly the entire championship injured, an inflamed ankle in one case, a swollen knee in the other, and not a complaint was heard from either.

Now, at the end of the match, they didn't know if they should give each other a slug or a hug.

Years later, I asked Obdulio, "Do you ever see Zizinho?"

"Sure. Once in a while," he said. "We close our eyes and we see each other."

July 17

The Queen said:

"There's the King's Messenger. He is in prison now and being punished and the trial doesn't even begin till next Wednesday: and of course, the crime comes last of all."

"Suppose he never commits the crime?" said Alice.

—From *Alice Through the Looking-Glass*,
sequel to *Alice in Wonderland* by Lewis Carroll, 1872

July 18

HISTORY IS A ROLL OF THE DICE

One hundred and twenty years it took to build the temple to the goddess Artemis in Ephesus, one of the wonders of the world.

In a single night in the year 356 BC it was reduced to ashes.

No one knows who built the temple. The name of its assassin, however, still resounds. Herostratus, the arsonist, wanted to go down in history. And he did.

July 19

The First Tourist on Rio's Beaches

Portuguese Prince-Regent João, son of Queen Maria, visited the beach at the port of Rio de Janeiro on his doctor's advice in 1810.

The monarch jumped into the water with his shoes on, wearing a barrel. He was terrified of crabs and waves.

His audacious example did not catch on. The beaches of Rio were noxious garbage dumps, where at night slaves deposited the waste of their masters.

By the time the twentieth century rolled around, the waters offered a much better swim, but take note: ladies and gentlemen were kept well apart, as the rules of modesty required.

One had to dress up to go to the beach. On shores that today are a geography of nudity, the he's went in covered to below the knees, and the pallid she's swaddled head to foot for fear the sun would turn them into mulattas.

July 20

In 1950 a photograph published in *Life* magazine caused a stir in New York's artistic circles.

The top painters of the city's avant-garde appeared together for the first time: Mark Rothko, Jackson Pollock, Willem de Kooning and eleven other masters of abstract expressionism.

All men, except for an unknown woman in a black coat and a little hat, with a bag on her arm, standing in the back row.

The men could not hide their disgust at her outrageous presence.

One tried, in vain, to excuse the interloper. He praised her saying, "She paints like a man."

Her name was Hedda Sterne.

July 21

The Other Astronaut

On this day in 1969, every newspaper in the world had the photo of the century on the front page: astronauts, lumbering like bears, had walked on the moon and left behind the first human footprints.

But the principal protagonist of the feat did not receive the congratulations he deserved.

Werner von Braun had designed and launched their spaceship.

Before taking up the conquest of space on behalf of the United States, von Braun had worked on Germany's behalf for the conquest of Europe.

Engineer, officer of the SS, he was Hitler's favorite scientist.

The day after the war ended, he used his smarts to make a prodigious leap and land on his feet on the other side of the sea.

He became an instant patriot of his new homeland, began worshipping at a Texas evangelical church and got busy in the space lab.

July 22

THE OTHER MOON

The astronauts weren't the first.

Eighteen hundred years before, Lucian of Samosata visited the moon.

No one saw him, no one believed him, but he wrote about it in Greek.

Back around the year 150, Lucian and his sailors set off from the Pillars of Hercules, where the Strait of Gibraltar now lies, and a storm caught the ship, whirled it up into the sky and dumped it on the moon.

On the moon, no one died. The oldest of the old lunatics dissolved into thin air. They ate smoke and sweated milk. The rich ones wore glass clothing, the poor no clothing at all. The rich had many eyes and the poor, one or none.

In a mirror the lunatics watched all the terrestrial comings and goings. For the duration of their visit, Luciano and his sailors kept tabs on the daily news from Athens.

July 23

TWINS

In 1944, in the tourist resort of Bretton Woods, it was confirmed that the twin brothers humanity needed were in gestation.

One was to be called International Monetary Fund and the other World Bank.

Like Romulus and Remus, the twins were nursed by a she-wolf until they took up residence in the city of Washington, cheek by jowl with the White House.

Ever since, these two govern the governments of the world. In countries where no one elected them, the twins impose obeisance as if it were destiny: they keep watch, they threaten, they punish, they quiz: "Have you behaved yourself? Have you done your homework?"

July 24

Sinners Be Damned

In the Aramaic language spoken by Jesus and his apostles, the same word means both "debt" and "sin."

Two millennia later, the debts of the poor merit the severest of punishments. Private property punishes those deprived of property.

July 25

RECIPE FOR SPREADING THE PLAGUE

In the fourteenth century fanatical custodians of the Catholic faith declared war on cats in Europe's cities.

These diabolical animals, instruments of Satan, were crucified, skewered, skinned alive or chucked into bonfires.

Then the rats, liberated from their worst enemies, came to rule the cities. And the Black Death, transmitted by rats, killed thirty million Europeans.

July 26

It's Raining Cats

On the big island of Borneo, cats used to eat the lizards that ate the cockroaches, and the cockroaches ate the wasps that ate the mosquitoes.

DDT was not on the menu.

In the middle of the twentieth century, the World Health Organization bombarded the island with massive doses of DDT to fight malaria, and they annihilated the mosquitoes and everything else.

When the rats found out that the cats had been poisoned, they invaded the island, devoured the fruit of the fields and spread typhus and other calamities.

Faced with the unforeseen rat attack, the experts of the World Health Organization convened a crisis committee and decided to parachute in cats.

Around this time in 1960, felines by the dozen descended from the skies over Borneo.

The cats landed softly, to the cheers of the humans who had survived the assistance of the international community.

July 27

The Locomotive from Prague

Today in Helsinki, the 1952 Olympics came to an end.

Emil Zatopek, unbeatable long-distance runner, as strong and speedy as a locomotive, won three gold medals.

In his country he was declared a national hero and given the rank of colonel in the Czechoslovakian army.

Some years later, in 1968, Zatopek supported the popular uprising and opposed the Soviet invasion.

The colonel became a street sweeper.

July 28

In 1890, in a letter to his brother Theo, Vincent van Gogh wrote:

Let my paintings speak.

He killed himself the following day.
His paintings speak for him still.

July 29

We Want a Different Time

For three days in 1830, six thousand barricades turned the city of Paris into a battlefield and defeated all the king's soldiers.

When this day became night, crowds used stones and bullets to smash the city's clocks: the grand clocks of the churches and other temples of power.

July 30

International Friendship Day

As Carlos Fonseca Amador liked to say, a friend criticizes you to your face and praises you behind your back.

And as experience says, a real friend is a friend in all seasons. The others are just summertime friends.

July 31

TIME FORETOLD

In ancient times there was an uprising of things.

As the Mayas know, before the before, all the mistreated kitchen implements rebelled: burnt pans, chipped mortars, nicked knives, broken crockery. And the gods supported them in their rebellion.

Much later, on the plantations of Yucatán, Maya slaves, who were treated as things, rose up against the masters who gave orders by whip, because they said Indians had their ears on their backs.

On this night in 1847, war broke out. For half a century slaves would occupy the plantations, and they burned the documents that legalized their enslavement and the enslavement of their children and the enslavement of their children's children.

AUGUST

August 1

OUR MOTHER WHO ART IN EARTH

Today in the towns of the Andes, Mother Earth, Pachamama, celebrates her big fiesta.

Her children sing and dance on this everlasting day, and they share with Mother Earth a mouthful of every corn delicacy, and a sip of each of the strong drinks that lubricate their joy.

At the end they ask forgiveness for the harm the despoiled and poisoned earth has suffered, and they plead with her not to punish them with earthquakes, frosts, droughts, floods or other furies.

This is the oldest faith in the Americas.

Here is how the Tojolobal Mayas of Chiapas greet our Mother:

> *You offer us beans,*
> *which are so delicious*
> *with hot peppers, with tortilla.*
>
> *Corn you give us, and fine coffee.*
> *Dear mother,*
> *take good care of us, do.*
> *And may it never occur to us*
> *to put you up for sale.*

She does not live in heaven. She lives in the depths below ground, and there she awaits us: the earth that feeds us will feed on us in turn.

August 2

Champ

On this day in 1980, Colombian boxer Kid Pambelé, out cold on the canvas, lost his world title.

He was born in Palenque, the old refuge for rebel slaves, and before becoming world champion he sold newspapers, shined shoes and boxed in little towns lost on the map in return for food.

Eight years his glory lasted. More than a hundred bouts, only twelve defeats.

He ended up throwing punches at his own shadow.

August 3

THE BELOVEDS

This story began when the gods, envious of human passion, punished Zhinü the weaver and her lover, whose name has been forgotten. The gods severed their embrace, which had made them one, and condemned each to solitude. Ever since, they live on either side of the Milky Way, the great celestial river that cannot be crossed.

But once a year and for one night only, on the seventh night of the seventh moon, what was rent can be sewn.

Magpies lend a hand, or rather a wing. Linking wings, they form a bridge for the nighttime encounter.

Weavers, embroiderers and tailors from all over China are on pins and needles, praying it will not rain.

If it does not, the weaver Zhinü gets under way. The dress she slips on and will soon slip off is the work of her masterful hands.

But if it rains, the magpies will not come, no bridge across the heavens will knit up what has been unraveled, and on earth no festival will celebrate the art of loom and needle.

August 4

CLOTHING TELLS THE TALE

Some two thousand years ago the great city of the Miaos was razed.

As ancient Chinese manuscripts reveal, somewhere in the vast plains between the Yellow and Yangtze Rivers, lay a city where "people with wings who called themselves the Miaos lived."

There are nearly ten million Miaos in China today. They speak a language that was never written down, but they dress in clothing that speaks of their lost grandeur. With silk threads they weave the story of their origins and their exodus, their births and their burials, wars of gods and of men, and also the monumental city that no longer is.

"We wear the city," one of the oldest of them explains. "The gate is in the cowl. The streets run all over the cloak, and on the shoulders our gardens grow."

August 5

The Liar Who Was Born Thrice

In 1881, when Pinocchio was no more than two months old, he was already an idol among Italy's children.

The book that narrated his adventures sold like candy.

Pinocchio was created by the carpenter Geppetto, who in turn was created by the writer Carlo Collodi. As soon as Geppetto made his hands, pinewood hands, the doll pulled off the carpenter's wig and revealed his bald pate. No sooner had he made his legs than Pinocchio took off running to complain to the police.

Collodi was fed up with the shenanigans of this mischievous brat and decided to hang him. He left him swinging from a holm oak.

Soon enough, besieged by the children of all Italy, Collodi had to bring him back to life. That was his second birth.

The third birth was a few years in coming. In 1940 Walt Disney stirred up a jam of honey and tears in Hollywood and resurrected Pinocchio, miraculously made good.

August 6

God's Bomb

In 1945, while this day was dawning, Hiroshima lost its life. The atomic bomb's first appearance incinerated this city and its people in an instant.

The few survivors, mutilated sleepwalkers, wandered among the smoking ruins. The burns on their naked bodies carried the stamp of the clothing they were wearing when the explosion hit. On what remained of the walls, the atom bomb's flash left silhouettes of what had been: a woman with her arms raised, a man, a tethered horse.

Three days later, President Harry Truman spoke about the bomb over the radio.

He said: "We thank God that it has come to us, instead of to our enemies; and we pray that He may guide us to use it in His ways and for His purposes."

August 7

Spy On Me

Mata Hari was born on this day in 1876.

Sumptuous beds were her battlefields in World War I. Top military and political leaders succumbed to her charms, and they confided secrets she then sold to France or Germany or whomever would pay more.

In 1917 a French military court condemned her to death.

The most beloved spy in the world blew kisses to the firing squad.

Eight of the twelve soldiers missed.

August 8

CURSED AMERICA

Today in 1553 marked the end of Girolamo Fracastoro's life. The Italian physician and writer had researched syphilis, among other contagious diseases, and concluded that the malady did not come to Europe from the Indians of the Americas.

In our time, Moacyr Scliar, Fracastoro's Brazilian colleague in science and letters, continued demolishing the myth of the supposed "American curse."

Long before the conquest of the New World, the French called syphilis "the Italian disease," and the Italians called it "the French disease."

The Dutch and the Portuguese called it "the Spanish disease."

It was "the Portuguese disease" for the Japanese, "the German disease" for the Polish and "the Polish disease" for the Russians.

And the Persians believed it came from the Turks.

August 9

Rigoberta Menchú was born in Guatemala four centuries and a half after the conquest by Pedro de Alvarado, and five years after Dwight Eisenhower conquered it once more.

In 1982, when the army swept through the Mayas' highlands, nearly all of Rigoberta's family was wiped out. Erased from the map was the village where her umbilical cord had been buried so she would set down roots.

Ten years later, she received the Nobel Peace Prize. She declared: "I receive this prize as an homage to the Maya people, even though it arrives five hundred years late."

The Mayas are a patient people. They have survived five centuries of butchery.

They know that time, like a spider, weaves slowly.

August 10

All men. But one was a woman, Manuela Cañizares, who recruited the others and brought them to her home to conspire.

On the night of August 9, 1809, the men spent hours and hours arguing—yes, no, who knows—and could not agree on whether to proclaim Ecuador's independence. When once more they postponed the matter for another occasion, Manuela faced them and shouted, "Cowards! Wimps! You were born to be servants!" And at dawn today the door of a new era opened.

Another Manuela, Manuela Espejo, also an early promoter of independence, was Ecuador's first female journalist. Since such a career was not proper for ladies, she used a pseudonym to publish her audacious articles against the servile mentality that humiliated her country.

Yet another Manuela, Manuela Sáenz, will always be known as Simón Bolívar's lover, but she was also herself: a woman who fought against the colonial power and male omnipotence and the hypocritical prudery of each.

August 11

FAMILY

As people know in black Africa and indigenous America, your family is your entire village with all its inhabitants, living or dead.

And your relatives aren't only human.

Your family also speaks to you in the crackling of the fire,
in the murmur of running water,
in the breathing of the forest,
in the voices of the wind,
in the fury of thunder,
in the rain that kisses you
and in the birdsong that greets your footsteps.

August 12

Athletes Male and Female

In 1928 the Amsterdam Olympics came to an end.

Tarzan, alias Johnny Weissmuller, was the swimming champ and Uruguay the soccer champ. For the first time the Olympic flame, alight in a tower, burned throughout the competition, from beginning to end.

These games were memorable for another novelty: women took part.

Never in the entire history of the Olympics, from Greece onward, had there been anything like it.

In ancient Greece, not only were women banned from competition, they could not even attend as spectators.

The founder of the modern Olympics, Baron de Coubertin, opposed the presence of women as long as his reign lasted: "For women, grace, home and children. For men, competitive sports."

August 13

The Right to Bravery

In 1816 the government in Buenos Aires bestowed the rank of lieutenant colonel on Juana Azurduy "in virtue of her manly efforts."

She led the guerrillas who took Cerro Potosí from the Spaniards in the war of independence.

War was men's business and women were not allowed to horn in, yet male officers could not help but admire "the virile courage of this woman."

After many miles on horseback, when the war had already killed her husband and five of her six children, Juana also lost her life. She died in poverty, poor even among the poor, and was buried in a common grave.

Nearly two centuries later, the Argentine government, now led by a woman, promoted her to the rank of general, "in homage to her womanly bravery."

August 14

The Mosquito Maniac

In 1881 Cuban physician Carlos Finlay demonstrated that yellow fever, also known as black vomit, was transmitted by a certain female mosquito. At the same time, he unveiled a vaccine that could eradicate the disease.

Carlos, known in the neighborhood as "the Mosquito Maniac," spoke of his discovery before the Academy of Medical, Physical and Natural Sciences of Havana.

It took twenty years for the rest of the world to find out.

During those twenty years, while prestigious scientists in prestigious places followed false leads, yellow fever continued its deadly ways.

August 15

The Jewel and the Crown

Winston Churchill proclaimed:

"It is alarming and also nauseating to see Mr. Gandhi . . . this malignant subversive fanatic . . . The truth is that Gandhiism and all it stands for will, sooner or later, have to be grappled with and finally crushed. It is no use trying to satisfy a tiger by feeding him cats' meat . . . We have no intention of casting away the most truly bright and precious jewel in the Crown of the King, which more than all our other Dominions and Dependencies constitutes the glory and strength of the British Empire."

Fifteen years later, the jewel abandoned the crown. On this day in 1947, India won its independence.

The hard road to freedom began in 1930 when Mahatma Gandhi, skinny and half-naked, reached a beach on the Indian Ocean.

It was the salt march. They were only a few when the march began, but a multitude by the time they got there. Each of them picked up a pinch of salt from the beach and brought it to his mouth, and thus broke the British law that forbade Indians from consuming salt from their own country.

August 16

SUICIDE SEEDS

For about three hundred and sixty million years, plants have been producing fertile seeds that generate new plants and new seeds, and never have they ever charged anyone for the favor.

But in 1998 a patent gave its blessing to the company Delta and Pine to produce and sell sterile seeds, which meant new seeds had to be purchased for every planting. In the middle of August of the year 2006, Monsanto, blessed be thy name, bought out Delta and Pine and also its patent.

Thus Monsanto consolidated its universal power: sterile seeds, known as "suicide seeds" or "terminator seeds," form part of a very lucrative line that also obliges farmers to buy herbicides, pesticides and other poisons from the genetically modified pharmacy.

At Easter in the year 2010, a few months after the earthquake, Haiti received a grand gift from Monsanto: sixty thousand bags of seed produced by the chemical industry. Farmers gathered to receive the offering, and they burned every sack in an immense bonfire.

August 17

DANGEROUS WOMAN

Mae West, sinning flesh, voracious vampiress, was born in 1893.

In 1927 she and her entire entourage went to jail for having put on stage at a Broadway theater an invitation to pleasure, subtly titled *Sex*.

When she finished serving time for her "crime of public obscenity," she decided to move from Broadway to Hollywood, from stage to screen, believing that the kingdom of freedom was about to arrive.

But in 1930, to ward off government censorship, Hollywood invented its own certificate of moral correctness, which for thirty-eight years determined which movies could open and which could not.

The Hays Code sought to keep the movies free of nudity, suggestive dances, lustful kissing, adultery, homosexuality and other perversions that undermine the sanctity of marriage and family. Not even Tarzan's films escaped unscathed and Betty Boop had to put on a long skirt. Naturally, Mae West kept getting into trouble.

August 18

The Network of Networks

Around this time in 1969, a group of scientists in the US armed forces started up a new project: they were going to create a network of networks to connect and coordinate military operations on a scale never before seen.

In the war to conquer heaven and earth, this invention, not yet called the Internet, turned into a victory for the United States against its rival power, still called the Soviet Union.

Paradoxically, with the passing of the years, this instrument of war has also served to amplify the voices of peace, which previously resounded like a wooden bell.

August 19

War on the Chessboard

In 1575 the first important battle in the history of chess was fought.

The winner, Leonardo da Cutri, received a prize of a thousand ducats, an ermine cape and a letter of congratulations from King Philip II of Spain.

The loser, Ruy López de Segura, wrote the book that founded the art of black–white combat on the checkered field. In that work the author, a cleric, beatifically advised:

> When you sit down to play, if it is a clear and sunny day, make sure the enemy has the sun in his face, because it will blind him. And if it is dark and you are playing with lamps, put the light on his right because it will bother his eyes and cast a shadow when he reaches his right hand over the board, so he will have a hard time seeing where he is moving the pieces.

August 20

HEAVEN'S WORKFORCE

In the Ecuadorian highlands stands the church of Licto.

This fortress of the faith was reconstructed using gigantic stones, as the twentieth century came into being.

Since slavery was long gone, or so said the law, free Indians took up the task: they carried the stones on their backs from a quarry several leagues distant, and several of them lost their lives walking those narrow paths alongside deep gorges.

The priests charged sinners in stones for their salvation. Every baptism was paid for with twenty, and a wedding cost twenty-five. Fifteen stones was the price of a burial. If the family did not deliver them, the deceased could not enter the cemetery; he was buried in "evil land" and from there went straight to hell.

August 21

The Division of Labor

At Stanford University in the United States psychologists carried out a revealing experiment on the relationship between man and function.

They recruited a few students, white, well-educated, well-behaved and in good physical and mental health.

The toss of a coin decided who would be the jailer and who the prisoner in a fictitious jail set up in the basement of a university building.

The prisoners, unarmed, were numbers without names. The jailers, names without numbers, carried nightsticks.

It seemed like a game, but from the very first day those playing the role of jailer began to enjoy its pleasures. Permission to use the toilet was given only after much begging, prisoners were obliged to sleep naked on the concrete floor, and those who protested paid for their insolence in punishment cells, deprived of food and water.

Blows, insults, humiliations: the experiment did not last long. No more than a week. On this day in 1971, it ended.

August 22

THE BEST WORKERS

The French priest Jean-Baptiste Labat recommended in one of his books published in 1742:

> African ten-to-fifteen-year-olds are the best slaves to take to America. The advantage is you can educate them so that they'll keep up the pace as best suits their masters. Children more easily forget their native countries and the vices that hold sway there, they become fond of their masters and they are less inclined to rebel than older blacks.

This pious missionary knew what he was talking about. On the French islands of the Caribbean, Père Labat performed baptisms, communions and confessions, and between masses kept an eye on his properties. He owned lands and slaves.

August 23

THE IMPOSSIBLE COUNTRY

In 1791 another owner of lands and slaves sent a letter from Haiti: "The blacks are very obedient and will remain so always," it said.

The letter was making its way to Paris when the impossible happened: on the night of August 22, a stormy night, the greatest slave uprising in the entire history of humanity exploded from the depths of the Haitian jungle. And those "very obedient" blacks went on to humble the army of Napoleon Bonaparte that was soon to overrun Europe from Madrid to Moscow.

August 24

IT WAS THE DAY OF THE ROMAN GOD OF FIRE

And it was the year 79.

Pliny the Elder was sailing the world at the helm of a Roman fleet.

When he entered the Bay of Naples, he saw black smoke rising out of Vesuvius like a tall tree opening its branches to the sky. Suddenly night fell at noon, the world shook with violent tremors and a bombardment of fiery stones buried the carefree city of Pompeii.

A few years before, fire had razed the city of Lugdunum and Seneca had written: "A single night lay between the greatest city and none."

Lugdunum revived and is now called Lyon. Pompeii did not disappear; it lay intact under the ashes, preserved by the volcano that destroyed it.

August 25

THE IMPRISONED CITY IS RESCUED

At dawn on this day in 1944, Paris went crazy.

The Nazi occupation was over.

The first tanks and armored cars had entered the city a few hours before. "Is it the Americans?" people asked.

The names scrawled in white paint on those tanks and armored cars were: "Guadalajara," "Ebro," "Teruel," "Brunete," "Madrid," "Don Quijote," "Durruti" . . .

The first liberators of Paris were the Spanish Republicans.

Defeated in their own land, they had fought for France.

They were convinced that Spain's rescue would follow.

They were wrong.

August 26

PURITY OF THE FAITH

Ivan the Terrible was born on this day in 1530.

To educate the people in the Christian faith, in Moscow he built the great cathedral of Saint Basil, which remains the loveliest symbol of the city, and to perpetuate his Christian power he sent a few sinners to hell, his rivals, his relatives:

he set the dogs on Prince Andrei and Archbishop Leonid;

he burned Prince Pyotr alive;

with an ax he chopped up the princes Aleksandr, Repnin, Snuyon, Nikolai, Dmitri, Telepnev and Tyutin;

he drowned his cousin Vladimir in the river, as well as his sister-in-law Aleksandra and his aunt Eudoxia;

he poisoned five of his seven wives;

and with a blow from his cane he killed his son, his favorite, the one who bore his name, because the affront was too great.

August 27

PURITY OF THE RACE

In 1924 an imprisoned Adolf Hitler dictated his book *Mein Kampf*. On a day like today, he transmitted to the scribe what for him was the fundamental lesson of history:

> All the great cultures of the past perished only because the originally creative race died out from blood poisoning.

Fourteen years later, Benito Mussolini proclaimed in his *Manifesto of Race*:

> The purely European physical and psychological characteristics of Italians should not be altered in any way whatsoever. It is high time that the Italians declare themselves to be frankly racist.

August 28

"I Have a Dream"

On this day in 1963, before an immense crowd carpeting the vast open mall of Washington, the Reverend Martin Luther King Jr. dreamed out loud:

"I have a dream that my four children will one day live in a nation where they will not be judged by the color of their skin but by the content of their character. . . I have a dream that one day every valley shall be exalted, every hill and mountain shall be made low . . ."

At the time the FBI had declared King "the most dangerous Negro of the future in this nation," and numerous spies followed his every step, day and night.

But he continued denouncing racial humiliation and the Vietnam War, which turned black men into cannon fodder, and without any hesitation he said that his country was "the greatest purveyor of violence in the world."

In 1968 a bullet split his skull.

COLORED MAN

Beloved white brother:
When I was born, I was black.
When I grew up, I was black.
When I am in the sun, I am black.
When I fall ill, I am black.
When I die, I will be black.

And meanwhile you:
When you were born, you were pink.
When you grew up, you were white.
When you're in the sun, you turn red.
When you feel cold, you turn blue.
When you feel fear, you turn green.
When you fall ill, you turn yellow.
When you die, you will be gray.
So, which of us is the colored man?

—By Léopold Senghor,
poet of Senegal

August 30

DAY OF THE DISAPPEARED

Disappeared: graveless dead, nameless graves.
And also:
old-growth forests,
stars in city nights,
the fragrance of flowers,
the taste of fruit,
letters written by hand,
old cafés where there was time to waste,
soccer in the street,
the right to walk,
the right to breathe,
secure jobs,
secure retirement,
doors without locks,
a sense of community
and common sense.

August 31

HEROES

In 1943 during World War II, General George Patton harangued his soldiers:

"You are here because you are real men and all real men like to fight!

"Americans love a winner! Americans will not tolerate a loser! Americans despise cowards! Americans play to win all of the time! That's why Americans have never lost nor will ever lose a war!

"Americans pride themselves on being He Men and they are He Men!"

He must have been reincarnated. Before entering the US Army, he had been a warrior in Carthage and Athens, a gentleman at the court of England and a field marshal for Napoleon Bonaparte.

General Patton died at the end of 1945, run over by a truck.

SEPTEMBER

September 1

Traitors

A monument unveiled in Germany in the year 2009 honors soldiers who deserted.

Human history has left many memorials in its wake, but recognition such as this is certainly unusual.

An homage to traitors? Deserters are indeed traitors. What they betray is war.

September 2

The Inventor of Preemptive War

In 1939 Hitler invaded Poland because Poland was going to invade Germany.

While a million and a half German soldiers flooded the map of Poland and bombs poured down from German planes, Hitler explained his doctrine of preemptive war: prevention is better than treatment; I have to kill them before they kill me.

Hitler founded a school of military thought. From then on, preemptive is the claim made by all digestive wars, when countries devour countries.

September 3

A year after the invasion of Poland, Hitler had gobbled up half of Europe and was still on his headlong rampage. Austria, Czechoslovakia, Finland, Norway, Denmark, Holland, Belgium and France had already fallen or were about to fall, and the nightly bombings of London and other British cities were under way.

In its edition for today in 1940, the Spanish daily *ABC* reported that "one hundred and sixteen enemy planes" had been shot down, making no attempt to hide its satisfaction at "the great success of the Reich's attacks."

On the front page Generalissimo Francisco Franco smiled triumphantly. Gratitude was one of his virtues.

September 4

I GIVE MY WORD

In the year 1970, Salvador Allende won the election and was sworn in as president of Chile.

He said, "I will nationalize our copper mines."

And he said, "I won't get out of here alive."

He kept his word on both counts.

September 5

Fight Poverty: Kill Somebody Poor

King Louis XIV of France, the Sun King, was born today in 1638.

The Sun King dedicated his life to glorious wars against his neighbors and the meticulous care of his curled wig, his splendid capes and his high-heeled shoes.

Under his reign, two successive famines killed more than two million Frenchmen.

The figure is known thanks to the mechanical calculator invented by Blaise Pascal half a century before. Known too is the cause, thanks to Voltaire, who some time later wrote: "Good policy relies on this secret: knowing how to let die of hunger the people who allow the rest of us to live."

September 6

THE INTERNATIONAL COMMUNITY

The cook convened the calf, the suckling pig, the ostrich, the goat, the deer, the chicken, the duck, the hare, the rabbit, the partridge, the turkey, the dove, the pheasant, the hake, the sardine, the cod, the tuna, the octopus, the shrimp, the squid and even the crab and the turtle, who were the last to arrive.

When all were present and accounted for, the cook explained, "I have brought you here to ask what sauce you would like to be eaten with."

One of the invitees responded, "I don't want to be eaten at all."

The cook then adjourned the meeting.

September 7

The Visitor

About this time in the year 2000, one hundred and eighty-nine countries drew up the Millennium Declaration, by which they committed themselves to solving the world's most pressing problems.

Only one goal has been reached and it did not figure on their list: they managed to multiply the number of experts required to take on such a challenging agenda.

According to what I heard in Santo Domingo, one of those experts stopped by a chicken farm on the outskirts of the city belonging to Doña María de las Mercedes Holmes, and asked her, "If I tell you exactly how many chickens you have, will you give me one?"

He turned on his touch-screen tablet computer, initiated the GPS, connected with the satellite camera through his 3G cell phone and booted up the pixel-counting function.

"You have one hundred and thirty-two chickens."

And he caught one.

Doña María de las Mercedes did not leave it at that. "If I tell you what your work is, will you give me back my chicken? Okay, you're an international expert. I know because you came without anyone calling you, you entered my chicken farm without asking permission, you told me something I already knew and then you charged me for it."

September 8

The state of Sergipe, in Brazil's Northeast: Paulo Freire begins a new workday with a group of very poor peasant farmers he is teaching to read and write.

"How are you, João?"

João does not reply. He tugs on the brim of his hat. A long silence. Finally, he says, "I couldn't sleep. All night long I couldn't close my eyes."

No more words come, until he murmurs, "Yesterday, for the first time ever, I wrote my name."

September 9

José Artigas lived his life fighting astride a native pony and sleeping under the stars. When he governed the lands he freed, his throne was a cow's skull and his only uniform a poncho.

He went into exile with nothing but the clothes on his back, and he died in poverty.

Now, in Uruguay's most important square, an enormous bronze founding father mounted on a charging steed contemplates us from on high.

This triumphant champion decked out for glory is identical to every other statue of a venerable military hero the world over.

He claims to be José Artigas.

September 10

The First Land Reform in America

It happened in 1815 when Uruguay was not yet a country, not yet called Uruguay.

In the name of the people's rebellion, José Artigas expropriated "the lands of the bad Europeans and the worse Creole Americans," and ordered the land shared out among all.

It was the first land reform in America, half a century before Lincoln's Homestead Act and a century before Emiliano Zapata broke up Mexico's haciendas.

"A criminal act," the offended parties cried. Then to add insult to injury, Artigas informed them, "The least fortunate shall benefit most."

Five years later, a defeated Artigas marched into exile and in exile he died.

The lands were taken back from the least fortunate, but inexplicably the voices of the vanquished still say, "Nobody is better than anybody else."

September 11

A DAY AGAINST TERRORISM

Wanted: for kidnapping countries.

Wanted: for strangling wages and slashing jobs.

Wanted: for raping the land, poisoning the water and stealing the air.

Wanted: for trafficking in fear.

September 12

LIVING WORDS

On this day in 1921 Amilcar Cabral was born in the Portuguese colony of Guinea-Bissau, in West Africa.

He led the war of independence for both Guinea-Bissau and Cape Verde.

His words:

"Watch out for militarism. We are armed militants, not the military. None of this is incompatible with the joy of living."

"Ideas don't live in the head alone. They live also in the soul and the heart and the stomach and everywhere else."

"Learn from life, learn from our people. Hide nothing from our people. Tell no lies, expose them. Mask no difficulties, mistakes, failures. Claim no easy victories."

In 1973 Amilcar Cabral was assassinated.

He wasn't around to celebrate the independence of the countries he had worked so hard to bring about.

September 13

If I remember correctly, Sandokan, prince and pirate, the Tiger of Malaysia, was born in 1883.

Sandokan, like the other characters that kept me company as a child, materialized from the hand of Emilio Salgari.

Salgari was born in Verona and never sailed farther than the Italian coast. He never visited the Gulf of Maracaibo or the Yucatán jungle or the slave ports of the Ivory Coast. He never met the pearl fishermen of the Philippines or the sultans of the Orient or the pirates of the high seas or the giraffes of Africa or the buffaloes of the Wild West.

But thanks to him I was there, I met them.

When my mother wouldn't let me cross the street, Salgari's novels carried me across the seven seas and several seas more.

Salgari introduced me to Sandokan and to Lady Marianna, his impossible love, to Yanez the sailor, to the Black Corsair and to Honorata, daughter of the Corsair's enemy, and to so many other friends he invented so they would save him from hunger and keep him company in his solitude.

September 14

INDEPENDENCE AS PROPHYLACTIC

On this evening in 1821, a handful of gentlemen drew up the Declaration of Independence of Central America, which they solemnly signed the following morning.

The Declaration states, or more accurately confesses, that they had to declare independence without delay, "to prevent the terrible consequences that would result should the people declare it themselves."

September 15

Adopt a Banker!

In the year 2008, the New York Stock Exchange tanked.

Hysterical days, historical days: the bankers, those cleverest of bank robbers, had sucked their businesses dry, though none of them was ever caught on security camera and no alarm was ever tripped. By then a widespread crash was unavoidable. The collapse ricocheted around the world; even the moon was afraid of being laid off and having to relocate to another sky.

The magicians of Wall Street, experts at selling castles in the air, stole millions of homes and jobs, but only one of them went to prison. And when they hollered at the top of their lungs for help, for the love of God, their zeal was honored with the largest reward ever paid in human history.

That mountain of money would have fed all the hungry people in the world, dessert included, from here to eternity. The idea did not occur to anyone.

September 16

Costume Ball

At two in the morning on this day in 1810, Miguel Hidalgo shouted the cry that opened the way to Mexico's independence.

When that famous alarum was about to turn one hundred in 1910, the dictator Porfirio Díaz held the festivities a day early to coincide with his birthday, and he celebrated the centenary in a big way.

Mexico City, painted and polished, received distinguished invitees from thirty countries: top hats, feathered caps, fans, gloves, gold, silk, speeches . . . The Ladies Committee hid the beggars and shod the street kids. Indians were trousered gratis, while anyone wearing traditional homespun cotton was banned. Don Porfirio laid the cornerstone of Lecumberri Prison and solemnly inaugurated the Central Insane Asylum, with capacity for a thousand patients.

A stirring parade presented the nation's history. Hernán Cortés, the first of the many volunteers who came to improve the race, was played by a student from the dental school, and a glum-looking Indian marched in an Emperor Moctezuma costume. The crowd cheered loudest for the float that featured a French court in the style of Louis XVI.

September 17

MEXICO'S WOMEN LIBERATORS

The centenary celebrations were over and all that glowing garbage was swept away.

And the revolution began.

History remembers the revolutionary leaders Zapata, Villa and other he-men. The women, who lived in silence, went on to oblivion.

A few women warriors refused to be erased:

Juana Ramona, "la Tigresa," who took several cities by assault;

Carmen Vélez, "la Generala," who commanded three hundred men;

Ángela Jiménez, master dynamiter, who called herself Angel Jiménez;

Encarnación Mares, who cut her braids and reached the rank of second lieutenant hiding under the brim of her big sombrero, "so they won't see my woman's eyes";

Amelia Robles, who had to become Amelio and who reached the rank of colonel;

Petra Ruiz, who became Pedro and did more shooting than anyone else to force open the gates of Mexico City;

Rosa Bobadilla, a woman who refused to be a man and in her own name fought more than a hundred battles;

and María Quinteras, who made a pact with the Devil and lost not a single battle. Men obeyed her orders. Among them, her husband.

September 18

The First Female Doctor

This day in 1915 marked the end of Susan La Flesche Picotte's life.

At the age of twenty-five, Susan had become the first indigenous woman to graduate from medical school in the United States. Up to then, there had been no doctor at all on the reservation where the Omaha Indians eked out their lives.

Susan was the first and the only, the doctor for every person and every purpose, day and night, steadfast and alone in sun and snow. She combined medicine learned with knowledge inherited, college cures with granny's remedies, so that the lives of the Omahas would hurt less and last longer.

September 19

The First Female Admiral

The battle of Salamis ended five centuries before Christ.

Artemisia, the first female admiral in history, warned Persia's King Xerxes that the Strait of Salamis was the wrong place for the heavy Persian ships to battle the agile Greek triremes.

Xerxes paid no heed.

In the midst of the battle, when his fleet was getting roundly thrashed, he had no choice but to put Artemisia in command and thus save at least a few ships and some honor.

A red-faced Xerxes admitted, "My men have become women, and my women men!"

Meanwhile, far from there, a boy named Herodotus had his fifth birthday.

Some time later, he would tell this story.

September 20

In the year 2003 the fourth Women's World Cup took place.

At the end of the tournament, the Germans were the champions. In 2007 they won the world trophy a second time.

It was no walk down the garden path.

From 1955 to 1970 soccer had been forbidden to German women.

The German Football Association explained why: "In fighting for the ball feminine elegance vanishes, and both body and soul inevitably suffer damage. Displaying the body violates etiquette and decency."

September 21

PROPHET OF HIMSELF

Girolamo Cardano wrote treatises on algebra and medicine, found the solutions to several unsolvable equations, was the first to describe typhoid fever, researched the causes of allergies and invented several instruments still in use by navigators.

In his spare time he made prophecies.

When he did an astrological chart for Jesus of Nazareth that showed his fate had been written in the stars, the Holy Inquisition put him in prison.

Upon his release, Girolamo prophesied, "I shall die on September 21, 1576."

From that moment, he stopped eating.

And he hit the mark.

September 22

Car-free Day

Today, for one day, environmentalists and other irresponsible people want automobiles to disappear from the world.

A day without cars? Suppose it's contagious and that day becomes every day?

God doesn't want that and neither does the Devil.

Hospitals and cemeteries would lose their biggest clients.

The streets would be taken over by ridiculous cyclists and pathetic people on foot.

Lungs could no longer inhale the tastiest of poisons.

Feet, having forgotten how to walk, would trip over every pebble.

Silence would deafen all ears.

Highways would become depressing deserts.

Radio, television, magazines and newspapers would lose their most generous advertisers.

Oil-producing countries would face poverty.

Corn and sugar, now food for cars, would return to the humble human table.

September 23

Seafaring

They called her the Mulata de Córdoba, and no one knows why. She was a mulatta, but she was born in the port of Veracruz and lived there always.

They said she was a witch. Back around the year 1600 or so, the touch of her hands cured the ill and crazed the healthy.

Suspecting that she was possessed by the Devil, the Holy Inquisition locked her up in the fort on the island of San Juan de Ulúa.

In her cell she found a coal left behind from some long-ago fire.

With that coal she started doodling on the wall and her hand, wanting to without wanting to, drew a ship. And the ship broke free of the wall and carried the prisoner to the open sea.

September 24

THE INVENTOR MAGICIAN

In the year 1912 Harry Houdini showed off his new trick at the Busch Circus in Berlin:

The Chinese water torture cell!
The most original invention of all time!

It was a tank filled to the brim with water, then hermetically sealed after Houdini was lowered in upside down with his wrists and ankles shackled. Through glass, the audience could watch him under water, not breathing for what seemed like centuries, until the drowned man somehow managed to make his escape.

Houdini could not have known that many years later this form of asphyxiation would become the preferred torture of Latin America's dictatorships, or the one most praised by the expert George W. Bush.

September 25

Miguel Ignacio Lillo never went to college, but book by book he built a science library that filled his entire house.

On a day like today around 1915, a few students from Tucumán spent a long afternoon in that house of books, and they wanted to know how Don Miguel managed to keep them in such fine condition.

"My books breathe the air," the sage explained. "I open them. I open them and ask them questions. Reading is asking questions."

Don Miguel asked questions of his books and he asked many more of the world.

For the joy of asking questions, he traveled by horseback all over northern Argentina, step by step, hand's breadth by hand's breadth. That's how he learned secrets that the map conceals, old ways of speaking and living, birdsongs that cities ignore, wild pharmacies that display their wares in the open fields.

Not a few birds and plants were named by him.

September 26

What Was the World Like
When It Was Beginning to Be the World?

Florentino Ameghino was another inquisitive sage.

A paleontologist from childhood, he was still a boy in 1865, more or less, when he assembled his first prehistoric giant in a town in the province of Buenos Aires. On a day like today he emerged from a deep cave weighed down by bones, then in the street he started sorting jaws, vertebrae, hipbones . . .

"This is a monster from the Mesozoic Era," he explained to his neighbors. "Really ancient. You can't imagine how ancient."

And behind his back Doña Valentina, the butcher, could not keep from laughing: "But sonny . . . They're fox bones!"

And they were.

He was not discouraged.

Throughout his life he gathered sixty thousand bones from nine thousand extinct animals, real or imaginary, and he wrote nineteen thousand pages that won him the gold medal and a diploma of honor at the Paris Exposition.

September 27

Solemn Funeral

During the eleven presidencies of Antonio López de Santa Anna, Mexico lost half its territory and the president lost a leg.

Half of Mexico was gobbled up by the neighbor to the north after a couple of battles and in return for fifteen million dollars. The leg, lost in combat, was buried on this day in 1842 in Santa Paula Cemetery with full military honors.

The president, called Hero, Eagle, His Most Meritorious, Immortal Warrior, Founding Father, His Serene Highness, Napoleon of the West and the Mexican Caesar, lived in a mansion in Xalapa which looked a lot like the palace at Versailles.

The president had all the furniture brought from Paris, even the decorations and knickknacks. In his bedroom he hung an enormous curved mirror, which vastly improved the looks of whomever contemplated his image in it. Every morning upon rising he stood before the magic mirror and it showed him a gentleman: tall, dapper—and honest.

September 28

RECIPE FOR REASSURING READERS

Today is the international day devoted to the human right to information.

Perhaps a good opportunity to recall that, a month or so after atom bombs annihilated Hiroshima and Nagasaki, the *New York Times* discounted the rumors that were terrifying the world.

On September 12, 1945, the daily published a front-page story by its chief science reporter William L. Laurence, which challenged the alarmist notions head-on. There was no radioactivity whatsoever in those razed cities, the article assured one and all, it's only "the Japanese continuing their propaganda . . ."

That scoop won Laurence the Pulitzer Prize.

Sometime later it came out that he was receiving two monthly paychecks: one from the *New York Times*, the other from the payroll of the US War Department.

September 29

In 1948 Seretse Khama, the black prince of Botswana, married Ruth Williams, who was English and white.

No one was happy with the news. The British Crown, lord and master of much of black Africa, named a commission of inquiry to look into the matter. The wedding between two races sets a dangerous precedent, the Judicial Inquiry ruled. The commission's report was suppressed, and the couple was ordered into exile.

After his banishment, Khama came to lead the struggle for Botswana's independence. And in 1966 he became the country's first president, elected by a wide majority in a clean vote.

That was when he received, in London, the title of Sir.

September 30

From the south of Veracruz a boy set out to seek his fortune.

Upon his return years later, his father wanted to know what the boy had learned.

The son answered, "I am a translator. I learned the language of birds."

Then a bird sang and the father demanded, "If you aren't a damned liar, tell me what that bird said."

The son refused. He pleaded that he'd better not, that you wouldn't want to know, but his father would not relent. So he translated the bird's song.

The father grew pale. And he kicked his son out of the house.

OCTOBER

October 1

EMPTIED ISLAND

"There will be no indigenous population except seagulls," declared an internal British government memo.

And in 1966 they kept their word.

All the inhabitants of the island of Diego Garcia, minus the seagulls, were expelled under threat of bayonets and gunfire.

The British then leased the emptied island to the United States for half a century.

This paradise of white sand in the middle of the Indian Ocean became a military base, a station for spy satellites, a floating prison and torture chamber for suspected terrorists, and a staging ground for the annihilation of countries that deserve to be punished.

It also has a golf course.

October 2

THIS WORLD ENAMORED OF DEATH

Today, International Day of Nonviolence, let us recall the words of Dwight Eisenhower, who was not exactly a pacifist. In 1953, as president of the country that spends the most on weapons, he acknowledged:

"Every gun that is made, every warship launched, every rocket fired signifies, in the final sense, a theft from those who hunger and are not fed, those who are cold and are not clothed."

October 3

CURLING THE CURL

In 1905 German hairdresser Karl Nessler invented the permanent wave.

His experiments nearly incinerated the head of his long-suffering wife, a martyr to science, before Karl at last found the formula for making perfect curls and keeping them that way for two whole days in reality, and for several weeks in the advertising.

Then he took on a French name, Charles, to give his product some style.

Over time, curls became a privilege not only of women.

A few men dared.

We baldies did not.

October 4

Until some time ago, many Europeans thought animals were demons in disguise.

The execution of bedeviled beasts by hanging or by fire was a public spectacle as popular as the burning of Satan-loving witches.

On April 18, 1499, in the French abbey of Josaphat near Chartres, a three-month-old pig was tried in court.

Like all pigs, he had neither soul nor reason and was born to be eaten. But instead of being eaten he ate: he was accused of having had a child for lunch.

The charge was not based on any evidence.

Yet the little pig was still found guilty. Lacking proof, prosecuting attorney Jean Levoisier, a graduate in law and chief magistrate at the monastery at Saint-Martin de Laon, revealed that the devouring had taken place on Good Friday.

Then the judge passed sentence: capital punishment.

October 5

COLUMBUS'S FINAL VOYAGE

In 1992 the Dominican Republic finished building the most unusual lighthouse in the world, one so tall its beams disturb God's sleep.

The lighthouse was erected in homage to Christopher Columbus, the admiral who pioneered European tourism in the Caribbean.

Before the inaugural ceremony, Columbus's ashes were removed from Santo Domingo's cathedral and transported to a new mausoleum at the foot of the lighthouse.

While the ashes were en route, the president's younger sister Emma Balaguer died suddenly after touring the lighthouse, and the stage on which Pope John Paul II was to give his blessing collapsed.

Some malevolent minds considered this further proof that Columbus brings bad luck.

October 6

In 1547 when he felt death tickling his backside, Hernán Cortés instructed that he be buried in Mexico in the convent at Coyoacán, to be built in honor of his memory. When he died, the convent was still a maybe and the deceased was obliged to stay in a series of homes in Seville.

At last he found passage on a ship to Mexico, where he took up residence beside his mother in the church of San Francisco in Texcoco. From there, he moved on to another church to lie beside the last of his children, where he remained until the viceroy ordered him transferred in secret to the Hospital de Jesús out of reach of the Mexican patriots dying to ravage his tomb.

The key to the crypt went from hand to hand, priest to priest, for more than a century and a half, until not long ago forensic specialists confirmed that those awful teeth and syphilis-pocked bones were indeed what remained of the body of the conquistador of Mexico.

Of his soul, no one knows. They say Cortés had it consigned to a soul-keeper from Usumacinta, an Indian named Tomás, who caught souls fleeing on the final breath and kept them in a collection of little jars, but that could never be confirmed.

October 7

Pizarro's Final Voyages

The scientists who identified Hernán Cortés also confirmed that Francisco Pizarro resides in Lima. His is that pile of bones pierced by stakes and chipped by blows that tourists flock to.

Pizarro, a pig farmer in Spain and a marquis in America, was assassinated in 1541 by his fellow conquistadors when they fought heroically over the Incas' imperial booty.

He was quietly buried in the cathedral's front yard.

Four years later, they let him inside. He found a spot under the main altar until an earthquake hit and he went missing.

He remained missing for a long time.

In 1891 a crowd of admirers gawked at his mummy in a glass urn, though it quickly came out that the mummy was an impostor.

In 1977 workers repairing the cathedral crypt came upon a skull that once upon a time was said to belong to the hero. Seven years later a body came to join the skull, and Pizarro, complete at last, was moved with great pomp and ceremony to one of the cathedral's shining chapels.

Ever since, he has been on exhibit in Lima, the city he founded.

October 8

In 1967 seventeen hundred soldiers cornered Che Guevara and his handful of Bolivian guerrillas in a ravine called Quebrada del Yuro. Che was taken prisoner and murdered the following day.

In 1919 Emiliano Zapata was shot down in Mexico.

In 1934 Augusto César Sandino was slain in Nicaragua.

These three were the same age, about to turn forty.

These three Latin Americans of the twentieth century shared the same map and the same era.

And these three were punished for trying to make history instead of repeating it.

October 9

I Saw Him Seeing Me

In 1967, while Che Guevara was lying in the schoolhouse at La Higuera, murdered by order of Bolivia's generals and their distant commanders, a woman recounted what she had seen. She was one of many, a peasant among the many peasants who entered the school and walked slowly around the body.

"We walked over there and he looked at us. We walked over here and he looked at us. He was always looking at us. He was really nice."

October 10

The Godfather

My Sicilian friends tell me that Don Genco Russo, *capo dei capi* of the Mafia, arrived at the appointment a deliberate two and a half hours late.

In Palermo, in the Hotel Sole, Frank Sinatra waited.

On this midday in 1963, Hollywood's idol paid homage to the monarch of Sicily: Sinatra kneeled before Don Genco and kissed his right hand.

Throughout the world Sinatra was The Voice, but in the land of his ancestors more important than voice was silence.

Garlic, symbol of silence, is one of four sacred foods at the Mafia's table. The others are bread, symbolizing union; salt, emblem of courage; and wine, which is blood.

October 11

The Lady Who Crossed Three Centuries

Alice was born a slave in 1686 and remained a slave throughout her one hundred and sixteen years of life.

When she died in 1802, with her died a good part of the memory of Africans in America. Alice did not know how to read or write, but she was filled to the brim with voices that told and retold legends from far away and events lived nearby. Some of those stories came from the slaves she helped to escape.

At the age of ninety, she went blind.

At one hundred and two, she recovered her sight. "It was God," she said. "He wouldn't let me down."

They called her Alice of Dunks Ferry. Serving her master, she collected tolls on the ferry that carried passengers back and forth across the Delaware River.

When the passengers, all white, made fun of this ancient woman, she left them stuck on the other side of the river. They called to her, shouted at her, but she paid no heed. The woman who had been blind was deaf.

The Discovery

In 1492 the natives discovered they were Indians,
they discovered they lived in America,
they discovered they were naked,
they discovered there was sin,
they discovered they owed obedience to a king and a queen
from another world and a god from some other heaven,
and this god had invented guilt and clothing
and had ordered burned alive all who worshipped the sun and
the moon and the earth and the rain that moistens it.

October 13

ROBOTS WITH WINGS

Good news. On this day in the year 2011 the world's military brass announced that drones could continue killing people.

These pilotless planes, crewed by no one, flown by remote control, are in good health: the virus that attacked them was only a passing bother.

As of now, drones have dropped their rain of bombs on defenseless victims in Afghanistan, Iraq, Pakistan, Libya, Yemen and Palestine, and their services are expected in other countries.

In the Age of the Almighty Computer, drones are the perfect warriors. They kill without remorse, obey without kidding around, and they never reveal the names of their masters.

October 14

A Defeat for Civilization

In the year 2002, eight McDonald's restaurants closed their doors in Bolivia.

Barely five years had this civilizing mission lasted.

No one forced McDonald's out. Bolivians simply turned their backs, or better put, McDonald's turned their stomachs. The most successful company on the planet had generously graced the country with its presence, and these ingrates refused to acknowledge the gesture.

A distaste for progress dissuaded Bolivia from embracing either junk food or the dizzying pace of contemporary life.

Homemade empanadas derailed development. Bolivians, stubbornly attached to the ancient flavors of the family hearth, continue eating without haste in long, slow ceremonies.

Gone forever is the company that everywhere else makes children happy, fires workers who try to unionize and jacks up the rate of obesity.

October 15

Born from Corn

In the year 2009 the Mexican government authorized "experimental and limited" planting of genetically modified corn.

A clamor of protest arose from the countryside. Everyone knew the wind would spread this invasion far and wide, turning GMO corn into an unavoidable fate.

Many of the first villages of the Americas had been raised on corn: corn was people, people were corn, and corn, like people, came in all sorts of colors and flavors.

Will the children of corn, those whom corn begat, manage to resist the chemical industry's mad dash to impose its poisonous dictatorship on the world? Or will we end up accepting throughout the Americas this merchandise that calls itself corn but comes in only one color and has no flavor and no memory?

October 16

He Believed Justice Was Just

The English jurist John Cooke defended those no one else would and attacked the ones no one else could.

Thanks to him, for the first time in history the divine rights of kings bowed before the law of humans: in 1649, as lead prosecutor, Cooke charged King Charles I and convinced the jury with his well-argued case. The king was convicted of the crime of tyranny and the executioner cut off his head.

A few years later, the lawyer paid for his deed. He was accused of regicide and locked up in the Tower of London. He defended himself saying, "I simply applied the law."

That mistake cost him his life. Every attorney knows that the law smiles at those above and spits on those below.

Today in 1660 Cooke was hanged, drawn and quartered in the very room where he had challenged royal power.

October 17

Silent Wars

Today is International Day for the Eradication of Poverty. Poverty does not explode like bombs or boom like gunfire.

We know everything about poor people: what they don't work at, what they don't eat, how much they don't weigh, how much they don't grow, what they don't think, how often they don't vote, and what they don't believe in.

The only thing left to learn is why poor people are poor.

Could it be because we are clothed by their nakedness and nourished by their hunger?

October 18

Women Are Persons

Today in the year 1929, the law acknowledged for the first time that the women of Canada are persons.

Up to then, women thought they were, but the law disagreed.

The legal definition of persons did not include women, so the Supreme Court had decreed.

Emily Murphy, Nellie McClung, Irene Parlby, Henrietta Edwards and Louise McKinney drank tea and conspired.

And they trounced the Supreme Court.

October 19

Two thousand five hundred years ago, at dawn on a day like today, Socrates took a stroll around Piraeus with Glaucon, Plato's older brother.

Glaucon told the story of a shepherd from the kingdom of Lydia who once found a ring, slipped it on his finger and realized that no one could see him. The magic ring made him invisible in the eyes of all others.

Socrates and Glaucon philosophized lengthily on the moral of the story. But neither of the two wondered why women and slaves were invisible in Greece even though they never used magic rings.

October 20

The Prophet Yale

In 1843 Linus Yale, inspired by something the Egyptians invented four thousand years before, patented the most invulnerable lock ever made.

Yale went on to secure the doors and gates of nearly every country, and became the greatest defender of property rights in the world.

These days, cities ill with fright are nothing but gigantic locks. Few hands hold the keys.

October 21

THOU SHALT BLOW ONE ANOTHER UP

Back around the year 630 or so, a renowned Chinese physician and alchemist named Sun Simiao mixed potassium nitrate, saltpeter, sulfur, charcoal, honey and arsenic. He was seeking the elixir of eternal life; he discovered an instrument of death.

In 1867 the Swedish chemist Alfred Nobel patented dynamite in his country.

In 1876 he patented gelignite, better known as blasting jelly.

In 1895 he established the Nobel Peace Prize. As its name indicates, the prize rewards antiwar champions. It is financed with the fortune he harvested on the battlefields.

October 22

INTERNATIONAL DAY OF NATURAL MEDICINE

The Navajo Indians cure by chanting and painting.

Those medicinal arts, holy breath against unholy death, work alongside herbs, water and the gods.

Night after night for nine nights, the sick one listens to chants that frighten off the evil shadows in his body, while the painter's fingers paint in the sand: arrows, suns, moons, birds, rainbows, lightning bolts, serpents and everything else that helps heal.

When the curing ceremony is over, the patient returns home, the chants fade and the grains of painted sand blow away.

October 23

To Sing

On sweltering spring nights in the southern half of the world, male crickets call to the females.

They call by rubbing their four wings together.

Those wings don't know how to fly. But they know how to sing.

October 24

Scientists did not take him seriously. Antonie van Leeuwen-hoek had no Latin and no degree, and his discoveries were the fruit of happenstance.

To get a better look at the weaves of the fabric he sold, Antonie began experimenting with combinations of magnifying glasses, and by putting glass to glass he invented a five-hundred-lens micro-scope that in a drop of water revealed a multitude of microbes swimming as fast as they could.

Among other triflings, this cloth merchant discovered red blood cells, bacteria, spermatozoids, yeast, the life cycle of ants, the sexual life of fleas and the anatomy of bee stingers.

In the same city, Delft, in the same month of 1632, both Antonie and the painter Vermeer were born. And in that city each of them dedicated their lives to seeing the invisible. Vermeer sought the light hiding in shadows, while Antonie spied on the secrets of our most diminutive relatives in the kingdom of this world.

October 25

A Stubborn Man

It wasn't worth much in Colombia, the life of a man. That of a peasant practically nothing. The life of an Indian absolutely nothing. That of a rebel Indian less than nothing.

Nevertheless, inexplicably, in 1967 Quintín Lame died of old age.

He was born on this day in 1880 and lived his many years either in prison or in battle.

In Tolima, one of the scenes of his mishaps, he was jailed one hundred and eight times.

In the mug shots his eyes are always like stewed prunes from prison's first hello, and his head is shaved to sap his strength.

Landowners trembled at his name, and no doubt death feared him too. A man of soft speech and delicate gestures, Quintín walked the length and breadth of Colombia urging indigenous people to rebel.

"We have not come like unyoked pigs to stick our noses in somebody else's field. This land is our land," Quintín would say, and his tirades were history classes. He spoke of the past of that present, the why and the when of so much misfortune: knowing the before, lets you create a different after.

October 26

After twenty years of cannon fire and thousands upon thousands of dead Chinese, Queen Victoria sang her victory song: China, which had banned drugs, opened its doors to the opium sold by British merchants.

While the imperial palaces burned, Prince Gong signed the surrender in 1860.

It was a victory for freedom: freedom of commerce, that is.

October 27

War Against Drugs

In 1986 President Ronald Reagan took up the spear that Richard Nixon had raised a few years previous, and the war against drugs received a multimillion-dollar boost.

From that point on, profits escalated for drug traffickers and the big money-laundering banks;

more powerful drugs came to kill twice as many people as before;

every week a new jail opens in the United States, since the country with the most drug addicts always has room for a few addicts more;

Afghanistan, a country invaded and occupied by the United States, became the principal supplier of nearly all the world's heroin;

and the war against drugs, which turned Colombia into one big US military base, is turning Mexico into a demented slaughterhouse.

October 28

Simón's Folly

Today in 1769 in Caracas, Simón Rodríguez was born.

The Church baptized him as a *párvulo expósito,* a foundling, a child of no one, but he was the sanest child Hispanic America has ever known.

To punish his sanity, they called him "El Loco." He said that our countries were not free, even if they had anthems and flags, because free people don't copy, they create, and free people don't obey, they think. To really teach, El Loco liked to say, is to teach to question.

October 29

GOOD-HEARTED MAN

In 1981, in a gesture of generosity that honors his memory, General Augusto Pinochet gave away the rivers, lakes and subterranean waters of Chile for a few coins. Several mining companies, like Xstrata of Switzerland, and power companies, like Endesa of Spain and AES Gener of the United States, became owners in perpetuity of the country's mightiest rivers. Endesa received a watershed the size of Belgium.

Farmers and indigenous communities lost their rights to water and were obliged to buy it. Ever since, the desert grows ever larger, devouring fertile lands and emptying the countryside of people.

October 30

THE MARTIANS ARE COMING!

In 1938 spaceships landed on the coasts of the United States and the Martians launched their attack. They had ferocious tentacles, enormous black eyes that shot fiery rays and foaming V-shaped mouths.

Many horrified citizens took to the streets wrapped in wet towels to protect themselves from the poison gas the Martians emitted, and many more chose to shut themselves in behind locks and more locks, armed to the teeth, awaiting the final battle.

Orson Welles invented that extraterrestrial invasion and broadcast it over the radio.

The invasion was a lie, but the fear was real.

And the fear continued: the Martians turned into Russians, Koreans, Vietnamese, Cubans, Nicaraguans, Afghanis, Iraqis, Iranians . . .

October 31

The Grandparents of Editorial Cartoons

In the year 1517 German monk Martin Luther nailed his challenge to the door of All Saints Church at Wittenberg Castle.

Thanks to an invention called the printing press those words did not just stay put. Luther's theses crossed streets and squares and entered the homes, taverns and temples of Germany and beyond.

The Protestant faith was being born. Luther attacked the Church of Rome's ostentation and extravagance, the blatant sale of tickets to Paradise, the hypocritical chastity of priests and more.

His heresies spread not only by word. Also by image, which reached many more people since few could read but nearly all could see.

The engravings that helped spread Luther's protest, works of Lucas Cranach, Hans Holbein and other artists, were not, shall we say, kind: the pope appeared as a monstrous golden calf, or an ass with bosoms and a Devil's tail, or an obese man covered in jewels falling head first into the flames of hell.

Without intending to, these sharp instruments of religious propaganda paved the way for the editorial cartoons of our day.

NOVEMBER

November 1

DANGER! ANIMALS!

In 1986 Mad Cow disease struck the British Isles and more than two million cows suspected of harboring contagious dementia faced capital punishment.

In 1997 avian flu from Hong Kong sowed panic and condemned a million and a half birds to premature death.

In the year 2009 Mexico and the United States suffered an outbreak of swine flu, and the entire world had to shield itself from the plague. Millions of pigs, no one knows how many, were sacrificed for coughing or sneezing.

Who is guilty of causing human disease? Animals.

It's that simple.

Free of all suspicion are the giants of global agribusiness, those sorcerer's apprentices who turn food into high-potency chemical bombs.

November 2

DAY OF THE DEAD

In Mexico tonight, as every year on this night, the living host the dead, and the dead eat and drink and dance and get caught up on all the latest gossip from the neighborhood.

But when night comes to a close, when church bells and first light bid them adieu, some of the dead get lively and try to hide in the shrubbery or behind the tombs in the graveyard. People chase them out with brooms: "Get going," "Leave us in peace," "We don't want to see you until next year."

You see, the dead are real layabouts.

In Haiti, a long-standing tradition forbids carrying the casket straight to the cemetery. The funeral cortege has to twist and turn and zigzag to fool the one who has died, so he won't be able to find his way back home.

The living minority defends itself as best as it can.

November 3

The Guillotine

Not only men lost their heads. Women, too, were decapitated and forgotten, since they weren't important like Marie Antoinette.

Three exemplary cases:

Olympe de Gouges was beheaded by the French Revolution in 1793 to remove her belief that women were citizens;

in 1943 Marie-Louise Giraud climbed the scaffold for having performed abortions, "criminal acts against the French family";

and the same year in Munich the guillotine sliced off the head of a student, Sophie Scholl, for handing out antiwar leaflets against Hitler. "Too bad," Sophie said. "Such a fine sunny day and I have to go."

November 4

The Suicide of Tenochtitlán

"Who could lay siege to Tenochtitlán?" the songs asked. "Who could move the foundations of heaven?"

In the year 1519 messengers reported to Aztec king Moctezuma that several strange beings were on their way to Tenochtitlán. They spit thunder and had metal breasts, hairy faces and six-legged bodies.

Four days later the monarch welcomed them.

They had arrived on the very same sea by which the god Quetzalcóatl had departed in ancient times, and Moctezuma believed that Hernán Cortés was the god returning. He said to him, "You have come home."

And he handed Cortés the crown and gave him offerings of gold: gold ducks, gold tigers, gold masks, gold and more gold.

Then, without unsheathing his sword, Cortés took the king prisoner in his own palace.

In the end, Moctezuma was stoned to death by his people.

November 5

A Sickness Called Work

In 1714 Bernardino Ramazzini died in Padua.

He was an unusual physician, who always began by asking, "What work do you do?"

That this might matter had never occurred to anyone before.

His experience allowed him to write the first treatise on occupational health, in which he described, one by one, the most common illnesses in more than fifty jobs. He demonstrated that there was little point in treating workers who must swallow their hunger and live deprived of sun and rest in shuttered workshops that are airless and filthy.

November 6

The King Who Was Not

King Charles II was born in Madrid in 1661.

During his forty years he never managed to stand up or speak without drooling or keep the crown from falling off his head, a head that never hosted a single idea.

Charles was his aunt's grandson, his mother was his father's niece and his great-grandfather was his great-grandmother's uncle: the Hapsburgs liked to keep things close to home.

So much devotion to family put an end to them.

When Charles died, the dynasty in Spain died with him.

November 7

One night in 1619, when René Descartes was still quite young, he dreamed all night long.

As he told it, in the first dream he was bent over, unable to straighten up, struggling to walk against a fierce wind that propelled him toward school and church.

In the second dream a bolt of lightning knocked him out of bed and the room filled up with sparks that illuminated everything in sight.

And in the third, he opened an encyclopedia, looking for a way to live his life, but those pages were missing.

November 8

LEGAL IMMIGRANTS

They flew to Monterrey in a private plane.

There, in the year 2008, they kicked off their triumphant tour. They were declared distinguished guests and were put on nine floats to tour the town.

It was as if they were politicians on a victory lap, but they weren't.

They were mummies, mummies from the cholera plague that devastated the city of Guanajuato more than a century and a half before.

The eleven women, seven men, five children and a bodiless head, all dressed for a party, then crossed the border. Though these mummies were Mexican, no one asked for their passports, nor did the border guards harass them.

They continued unimpeded to Los Angeles, Las Vegas and Chicago, where they paraded under flowered arches to cheering crowds.

November 9

On a day like today in 1989, the Berlin Wall met its end.

But other walls were born to keep the invaded from invading the invaders,

to keep Africans from collecting the wages the slaves never received,

to keep Palestinians from returning to the country stolen from them,

to keep Saharawis from entering their usurped land,

to keep Mexicans from setting foot on the immense territory bitten off from their country.

In the year 2005, the most famous human cannonball in the world, David Smith, protested in his own way the humiliating wall that separates Mexico from the United States. An enormous cannon shot him high into the Mexican air and David fell, safe and sound, on the forbidden side of the border.

He had been born in the United States but, while his flight lasted, he was Mexican.

November 10

Brazilian physician Drauzio Varella calculated that the world invests five times as much in male sex stimulants and female silicone implants as in finding a cure for Alzheimer's.

"In a few years," he prophesied, "we will have old women with huge tits and old men with stiff cocks, but none of them will remember what they are for."

November 11

FYODOR DOSTOEVSKY WAS BORN TWICE

The first time was in Moscow on this day in 1821.

He was born again at the end of 1849 in Saint Petersburg.

Dostoevsky had spent eight months in prison awaiting the firing squad. At first he hoped it would never happen. Then he accepted that it would happen when it happened. And in the end, he wanted it to happen right now, the sooner the better, because waiting was worse than dying.

Thus it went until early one morning when he and the other condemned men were dragged in chains to Semenovsk Square on the banks of the Neva.

The commanding voice shouted orders, and at the first command the gunmen blindfolded their victims.

At the second command, the click-clack of guns being cocked rang out.

At the third command of "Aim," there were pleas, moans, a few sobs. Then silence.

And silence.

And more silence. Until, in that silence without end, they were told that the tsar of all Russia, in a magnanimous gesture, had granted them a pardon.

November 12

I Don't Like It When They Lie to Me

Sor Juana Inés de la Cruz, born today in 1651, was the best. No one else flew so high in her place and her time.

She entered the convent very young, believing that it would be less of a prison than the home. She was misinformed. By the time she found out, it was too late. She died years later, having been condemned to silence, this the most articulate of women.

Her jailers liked to shower her with praise, which she never believed.

On one occasion a court painter, sent by the Mexican Viceroy, painted a portrait that was something like a forerunner of Photoshop. She replied:

> *This, in whom flattery has striven*
> *to pardon the years of their horrors,*
> *and vanquishing time of its rigors*
> *to defeat old age and oblivion,*
> *is a tedious mistaken errata,*
> *an empty yearning and, on close viewing,*
> *it's cadaver, dust, shadow, nada.*

November 13

The Father of Moby-Dick

In 1851 the first edition of *Moby-Dick* was published in New York.

Herman Melville, a pilgrim on land and sea, had written a few successful books, but *Moby-Dick*, his masterpiece, never sold out its first printing and the books that followed met with no better fate.

Melville died in obscurity, having learned that success and failure are accidents of doubtful importance.

November 14

The Mother of Female Journalists

On this morning in 1889, Nellie Bly set off.

Jules Verne did not believe that this pretty little woman could circle the globe by herself in less than eighty days.

But Nellie put her arms around the world in seventy-two, all the while publishing article after article about what she heard and observed.

This was not the young reporter's first exploit, nor would it be the last.

To write about Mexico, she became so Mexican that the startled government of Mexico deported her.

To write about factories, she worked the assembly line.

To write about prisons, she got herself arrested for robbery.

To write about mental asylums, she feigned insanity so well that the doctors declared her certifiable. Then she went on to denounce the psychiatric treatments she endured, as reason enough for anyone to go crazy.

In Pittsburgh when Nellie was twenty, journalism was a man's thing.

That was when she committed the insolence of publishing her first articles.

Thirty years later, she published her last, dodging bullets on the front lines of World War I.

November 15

Hugo Blanco Was Born Twice

The first time was in Cuzco in 1934.

Hugo Blanco arrived in a country split in two, Peru.

He was born somewhere in between.

He was white, but was raised in a town, Huanoquite, where the buddies he played and ran with spoke Quechua, and he went to school in Cuzco, where the sidewalks were reserved for decent folk, and Indians were not allowed on.

Hugo was born the second time when he was ten years old. In school he heard the news from his town that Don Bartolomé Paz had branded an Indian peon named Francisco Zamata with a red-hot iron. This owner of lands and people had seared his initials, BP, on the peon's ass because he hadn't taken good care of his cows.

The matter was not so uncommon, but it branded Hugo for life.

Over the years, this man who was not Indian became one. He organized peasant unions and paid the price for his self-chosen disgrace with beatings and torture, jail and harassment and exile.

On one of his fourteen hunger strikes, when he could go on no longer, the government was so moved it sent him a casket as a present.

An Examiner of Life

Being so nearsighted, he had no choice but to invent lenses that laid the foundations of modern optical science, as well as a telescope that discovered a new star.

And being a real gawker, he stared at a snowflake in the palm of his hand. He saw that its frozen soul was a six-pointed star, six, like the sides of the little cells in beehives. In his mind's eye he saw that the hexagonal form is the best use of space.

From the balcony of his house he discerned that the voyage of his plants in search of light was not circular, and he deduced that perhaps the voyage of the planets around the sun was not circular either. His telescope went on to measure the ellipses they describe on the sky.

He lived his life looking.

When he stopped seeing he died on this day in 1630.

The gravestone of Johannes Kepler says:

"I measured the heavens. Now the shadows I measure."

November 17

Brazilian composer Heitor Villa-Lobos died today in 1959.
He had two sets of ears, one facing in, the other facing out.

In the early years, when he earned his living playing piano in
a Rio de Janeiro whorehouse, Villa-Lobos found a way to concentrate on his opus: he closed his outer ears to the cacophony of guffaws and drunkenness, and he opened his inner ears to the music
being born, note by note.

Much later, those inner ears would become his refuge against
insults from the public and poison from the critics.

November 18

Zorro Was Born Four Times

For the first time in 1615. His name was William Lamport, and he was a redhead and Irish.

He was born again when he changed his name and his country. He became Guillén Lombardo, a Spaniard, captain of the Spanish Armada.

His third birth occurred when he became a hero of Mexico's long struggle for independence. In the year 1659, sentenced to die at the stake, he hanged himself rather than face the dishonor of being burned alive.

He was resuscitated in the twentieth century. In his fourth life he called himself Diego de la Vega and he wore a mask. He was Zorro, sword-fighting champion of the downtrodden, who left his mark with a "Z."

Douglas Fairbanks, Tyrone Power, Alain Delon and Antonio Banderas all wielded his sword in Hollywood.

November 19

The Moss and the Stone

At dawn on this day in 1915, Joe Hill faced a firing squad in Salt Lake City.

This foreign agitator, who had changed his name twice and his job and address a thousand times, had written the songs sung by striking workers all over the United States.

On his last night, he asked his comrades not to waste time crying for him:

> *My will is easy to decide,*
> *For there is nothing to divide.*
> *My kin don't need to fuss and moan,*
> *Moss does not cling to a rolling stone.*

November 20

THINGS CHILDREN SAY

Today is Children's Day.

I go for a stroll and bump into a girl who is two or maybe a little older, that age when we're all pagans.

The girl is skipping along, greeting all the greenery she sees: "Hello, grass!" "Good morning, grass!"

Then she stops to listen to the birds singing in the tops of the trees. And she applauds.

At noon on this day, a boy of about eight, maybe nine, brings a present to my house.

It's a folder filled with drawings.

The present comes from the students at a school in the Montevideo neighborhood of Cerrito de la Victoria. The young artist hands it to me with an explanation: "These drawings are us."

November 21

THE SADDEST MATCH IN HISTORY

In 1973 Chile was a country imprisoned by military dictatorship. The National Stadium had been turned into a concentration camp and torture chamber.

The Chilean national team was to play a decisive World Cup qualifying match against the Soviet Union.

Pinochet's dictatorship decided that the match had to be played in the National Stadium, no matter what.

The prisoners were hurriedly transferred and soccer's top brass inspected the field—the turf was impeccable—and gave their blessing.

The Soviet team refused to play along.

Eighteen thousand fans bought tickets and cheered the goal that Francisco Valdés put in the empty net.

The Chilean team played against no one.

November 22

International Music Day

As those with long memories tell it, in other times the sun was the lord of music, until the wind stole music away.

Ever since, birds console the sun with concerts at the beginning and end of the day.

But now these winged singers cannot compete with the screech and roar of the motors that rule big cities, and little or no birdsong can be heard. In vain they burst their breasts trying, and the effort ruins their trills.

Females no longer recognize their mates. The males, virtuoso tenors, irresistible baritones, do their best, but in the urban racket no one can tell who is whom, and the females end up accepting the embrace of unfamiliar wings.

November 23

Today in 1859 the first copy of Charles Darwin's *On the Origin of Species* rolled off the presses.

In the original manuscript the book had another name. It was called *Zoonomia*, in homage to a work by Charles's grandfather Erasmus Darwin.

Erasmus had fathered fourteen children and several books. Seventy years ahead of his grandson, he warned that everything in nature that sprouts, crawls, walks or flies has a common ancestor, and that common ancestor was not the hand of God.

November 24

Grandma

In 1974 her bones turned up in the rocky hills of Ethiopia. Her discoverers called her Lucy.

Thanks to advanced technology, they were able to calculate her age at about three million, one hundred and seventy-five thousand years, give or take a day or two. And also her height: she was rather short, a little over three feet tall.

The rest was deduced or maybe guessed: her body was quite hairy and she didn't walk on all fours, rather she swung along in a chimpanzee walk, her hands nearly grazing the ground, though she preferred the treetops.

She might have drowned in a river.

She might have been fleeing a lion or some other unknown who showed an interest in her.

She was born long before fire or the word, but perhaps she spoke a language of gestures and sounds that could have said, or tried to say, for example,

"I'm cold,"

"I'm hungry,"

"Don't leave me alone."

November 25

In the jungle of the Upper Paraná, the prettiest butterflies survive by exhibiting themselves. They display their black wings enlivened by red or yellow spots, and they flit from flower to flower without the least worry. After thousands upon thousands of years, their enemies have learned that these butterflies are poisonous. Spiders, wasps, lizards, flies and bats admire them from a prudent distance.

On this day in 1960 three activists against the Trujillo dictatorship in the Dominican Republic were beaten and thrown off a cliff. They were the Mirabal sisters. They were the prettiest, and they were called Las Mariposas, "The Butterflies."

In memory of them, in memory of their inedible beauty, today is International Day for the Elimination of Violence Against Women. In other words, for the elimination of violence by the little Trujillos that rule in so many homes.

Laura and Paul

When Karl Marx read *The Right to Be Lazy*, he concluded, "If that's Marxism, then I'm no Marxist."

The author, Paul Lafargue, seemed less a communist than an anarchist who harbored a suspicious streak of tropical lunacy.

Neither was Marx pleased at the prospect of having this not-very-light-complexioned Cuban for a son-in-law. "An all too intimate deportment is unbecoming," he wrote to him when Paul began making dangerous advances on his daughter Laura. And he added solemnly: "Should you plead in defense of your Creole temperament, it becomes my duty to interpose my sound sense between your temperament and my daughter."

Reason failed.

Laura Marx and Paul Lafargue shared their lives for more than forty years.

And on this night in the year 1911, when life was no longer life, in their bed at home and in each other's arms, they set off on the final voyage.

November 27

WHEN THE WATERS OF RIO DE JANEIRO BURNED

In 1910 the mutiny by Brazil's sailors reached its climax.

The rebels threatened the city of Rio de Janeiro with warning shots of cannon fire: "No more lashings or we'll turn the city to rubble."

On board warships, whippings were common fare and the victims frequently ended up dead.

After five days the uprising triumphed. The whips were sent to the bottom of the ocean, and the pariahs of the sea paraded to cheers through Rio's streets.

Sometime after that, the leader of the insurrection, João Cândido, child of slaves, admiral by acclaim of his fellow mutineers, went back to being a regular sailor.

Sometime after that, he was booted out of the service.

Sometime after that, he was arrested.

And sometime after that, he was locked away in an insane asylum.

There is a monument to him, a song explains, in the worn-down stones of the docks.

November 28

THE MAN WHO TAUGHT BY LEARNING

In the year 2009, the Brazilian government told Paulo Freire it was sorry. He was unable to acknowledge the apology since he had been dead for twelve years.

Paulo was the prophet of education for action.

In the beginning he taught classes under a tree. He taught thousands upon thousands of sugar workers in Pernambuco to read and write, so they could read the world and help to change it.

The military dictatorship arrested him, threw him out of the country and forbade his return.

In exile, Paulo wandered the world. The more he taught, the more he learned.

Today, three hundred and forty Brazilian schools bear his name.

November 29

WORLD TERROR CHAMPIONSHIP

In his scorn for human life, Hitler was unbeatable, but he had competitors.

In the year 2010 the Russian government officially acknowledged that Stalin had been the author of the murder of fourteen thousand five hundred Polish prisoners in Katyn, Kharkov and Miednoje. The Poles were shot in the back of the head in the spring of 1940, a crime always attributed to Nazi Germany.

In 1945, when the victory of the Allies was already inevitable, the German city of Dresden and the Japanese cities of Hiroshima and Nagasaki were razed to the last stone. The official version from the victorious powers maintained the cities were military targets, but the thousands upon thousands of dead were all civilians, and in the ruins not even a slingshot could be found.

November 30

A Date in Paradise

This day in the year 2010 saw the opening of a world conference to defend the environment, number one thousand and one.

As usual, nature's exterminators recited love poems to her.

It was held in Cancún.

No place could have been better.

At first sight Cancún is a picture postcard, but to transform this old fishing village into a gigantic trendy hotel with thirty thousand rooms, over the last half century dunes, lakes, pristine beaches, virgin forests and mangroves were wiped out, along with every other obstacle that nature put in the way of its path to prosperity. Even the beach sand was sacrificed. Now Cancún buys its sand from somewhere else.

DECEMBER

December 1

FAREWELL TO ARMS

Costa Rica's president Don Pepe Figueres once said: "Here, the only thing wrong is everything."

And in the year 1948 he disbanded the armed forces.

Many were those who decried it as the end of the world, or at least the end of Costa Rica.

But the world kept on turning, and Costa Rica was kept safe from wars and coups d'état.

December 2

INTERNATIONAL DAY FOR THE ABOLITION OF SLAVERY

In the middle of the nineteenth century, John Brown, a white traitor to his race and class, led an assault on a military arsenal in Virginia to get weapons for the slaves on the plantations.

Colonel Robert E. Lee commanded the troops that surrounded and captured Brown. Lee was promoted to general and soon came to lead the army that defended slavery during the long US war between the South and the North.

Lee, general of the slavers, died in bed. His send-off included military honors, martial music, cannon salutes and speeches that exalted the virtues of "the greatest military genius in America."

Brown, friend of the slaves, was convicted of murder, conspiracy and treason for his assault on the arsenal, and was sentenced to die. He was hanged on this day in 1859.

Today, which by coincidence is the International Day for the Abolition of Slavery.

December 3

THE KING WHO SAID "NO MORE"

For four centuries black Africa specialized in the sale of human flesh. In the international division of labor, Africa's fate was to produce slaves for the world market.

In 1720 one king refused.

Agaja Trudo, king of Dahomey, set fire to the Europeans' forts and razed the slave ports to the ground.

For ten years he fought off harassment from the traffickers and attacks from neighboring kingdoms.

He could hold out no longer.

Europe refused to sell him weapons if he did not pay in human coin.

December 4

GREEN MEMORIES

Like us, trees remember.

But unlike us, they do not forget: they grow rings in their trunks, one after another, to stockpile their memory.

The rings tell the story of each tree, revealing its age, as much as two thousand years in some cases, the climate it lived through, the floods and droughts it endured; the rings conserve the scars of fires, infestations and earthquakes.

One day like today, a scholar of the subject, José Armando Boninsegna, was given the best possible explanation by the children at a school in Argentina:

"Little trees go to school and learn to write. Where do they write? On their bellies. And how do they write? With rings that you can read."

December 5

The Longing for Beauty

The president of the Spanish Society of Natural History ruled in 1886 that the cave paintings at Altamira were not thousands of years old: "They are the work of some mediocre disciple of today's school of modern art," he insisted, confirming the suspicions of nearly all the experts.

Twenty years later, those experts had to admit they were wrong. Thus it was proven that the longing for beauty, like hunger, like desire, has always accompanied the human adventure in the world.

Many years before that thing we call civilization, we were turning bird's bones into flutes and seashells into necklaces, we were making colors by mixing earth, blood, powdered rocks and plant juices to beautify our caves and turn our bodies into walking paintings.

When the Spanish conquistadors arrived at Veracruz, they found the Huasteco Indians walking around naked, she's and he's, with their bodies painted to please each other and themselves.

"These are the worst," concluded the conquistador Bernal Díaz del Castillo.

December 6

On this day in 1938, the House Committee on Un-American Activities, operating out of Washington, questioned Hallie Flanagan.

She ran the Federal Theatre Project.

Joe Starnes, a congressman from Alabama, led the interrogation.

Referring to an article Hallie had written, he asked: "You are quoting from this Marlowe. Is he a Communist?"

"I am very sorry. I was quoting from Christopher Marlowe."

"Tell us who Marlowe is, so we can get the proper reference."

"He was the greatest dramatist in the period immediately preceding Shakespeare."

"Of course, we had what some people call Communists back in the days of the Greek theater."

"Quite true."

"And I believe Mr. Euripides was guilty of teaching class consciousness, wasn't he?"

"I believe that was alleged against all of the Greek dramatists."

"So we cannot say when it began," sighed Congressman Starnes.

December 7

ART DOESN'T AGE

In the year 1633, more or less on this day, Gregório de Matos was born, the poet who knew best how to poke fun at colonial Brazil.

In 1969, at the height of the military dictatorship, the commander of the Sixth Region denounced his poems as "subversive." They had been enjoying the sleep of the just for three centuries in the library of the Ministry of Culture in the city of Salvador da Bahia, when the commander threw them onto the bonfire.

In 1984, in a neighboring country, the military dictatorship of Paraguay banned a play about to open in the Harlequin Theater, since it was a "pamphlet against order, discipline, soldiers and the law." Twenty-four centuries had passed since Euripides had written *The Trojan Women*.

December 8

The Art of Neurons

In 1906 Santiago Ramón y Cajal received the Nobel Prize in medicine.

He had wanted to be a painter.

His father would not let him, so he had to become the greatest Spanish scientist of all time.

He got his revenge by sketching his discoveries. His drawings of the brain were on a par with Miró and Klee: "The garden of neurology sparks incomparable artistic emotions," he liked to say.

He enjoyed exploring the mysteries of the nervous system, but he loved drawing them even more.

And what he loved most of all was saying out loud whatever was on his mind, well aware that it would make him more enemies than friends.

Sometimes he would ask in surprise, "You have no enemies? How can that be? Did you never tell the truth or stand up for justice?"

December 9

The Art of Living

In 1986 the Nobel Prize for medicine went to Rita Levi-Montalcini.

In troubled times, during the dictatorship of Mussolini, Rita had secretly studied nerve fibers in a makeshift lab hidden in her home.

Years later, after a great deal of work, this tenacious detective of the mysteries of life discovered the protein that multiplies human cells, which won her the Nobel.

She was about eighty by then and she said, "My body is getting wrinkled, but not my brain. When I can no longer think, all I'll want is help to die with dignity."

December 10

BLESSED WAR

In the year 2009, on the anniversary of the signing of the Universal Declaration of Human Rights, President Barack Obama received the Nobel Peace Prize.

In his acceptance speech, the president thought it wise to pay homage to war: "times when nations will find the use of force not only necessary but morally justified."

Four and a half centuries before, when the Nobel Prize did not exist and evil resided in countries not with oil but with gold and silver, Spanish jurist Juan Ginés de Sepúlveda also defended war as "not only necessary but morally justified."

Ginés explained that war was necessary against the Indians of the Americas, "being by nature servile men who are barbarian, uncultured and inhuman," and that war was justified, "because it is just, by natural right, that the body obey the soul, that the appetite obey reason, that brutes obey man, women their husbands, the imperfect the perfect and the worse the better, for the good of all."

December 11

THE POET WHO WAS A CROWD

Fernando Pessoa, the poet from Portugal, believed he lived with five or six other poets inside him.

At the end of 2010 the Brazilian writer José Paulo Cavalcanti completed his many years of research on "someone who dreamed he was many."

Cavalcanti discovered that Pessoa did not contain five or even six: he had one hundred and twenty-seven guests in his capacious body, each with his own name, style and history, birth date and horoscope.

His one hundred and twenty-seven inhabitants signed poems, articles, letters, essays, books . . .

Several of them published vituperous criticisms of him, but Pessoa never kicked any of them out, even if it was not easy to keep such a large family fed.

December 12

Tonantzin Is Called Guadalupe

Long after giving birth to Jesus, the Virgin Mary traveled to Mexico.

She arrived on this day in the year 1531 and introduced herself as the Virgin of Guadalupe. By a fortunate coincidence her visit occurred precisely where Tonantzin, the Aztec mother god, had her temple.

From that moment on the Virgin of Guadalupe became the incarnation of the Mexican nation: Tonantzin lives on in the Virgin, and Mexico and Jesus share the same mother.

In Mexico, as everywhere else in Latin America, outlawed gods entered the Catholic divinities on currents of air and took up residence in their bodies.

Tlaloc brings rain as Saint John the Baptist, and as Saint Isidore the Laborer Xochipilli makes flowers bloom.

God the Father is Father Sun.

Tezcatlipoca, Jesus on the cross, points in the four directions from which the winds of the indigenous universe flow.

December 13

In 1589 Pope Sixtus V decided that castrated men should sing in Saint Peter's Basilica.

To enable male singers to become sopranos of high notes and unbroken trills, their testicles were mutilated.

For more than three centuries castrated men took the place of women in church choirs: the sinning voices of the daughters of Eve, which would have soiled the purity of the sanctuaries, were forbidden.

December 14

THE MONK WHO ESCAPED SEVEN TIMES

In 1794 the archbishop of Mexico, Alonso Núñez de Haro, signed the sentence condemning Father Servando Teresa de Mier.

On the anniversary of the visit of the Virgin Mary to Mexico, Father Servando had given a sermon before the viceroy, the archbishop and the members of the Royal Audience.

More than a sermon, it was a cannonball. Father Servando dared to affirm that there was nothing random or coincidental about it: the Virgin Mary *was* the Aztec goddess Tonantzin, and Thomas the Apostle *was* Quetzalcóatl, the plumed serpent worshipped by the Indians.

For having committed such scandalous blasphemy, Father Servando was stripped of his title of doctor in philosophy and was forbidden in perpetuity from teaching, hearing confession or giving sermons. And he was sentenced to exile in Spain.

From that point on, he was jailed seven times and seven times he escaped. He fought for Mexico's independence, wrote ferocious and funny attacks on the Spanish and penned serious treatises on his vision of a republic freed from colonial and military strictures—the Mexican nation as would be when it became its own lord and master.

December 15

Green Man

Today would have been the birthday of Chico Mendes.

Would have been.

But the assassins of the Amazon, who kill troublesome trees, also kill troublesome people.

People like Chico Mendes.

His parents, debt slaves, arrived in the rubber plantations from the far-off desert of Ceará.

He learned to read when he was twenty-four.

In the Amazon he organized unions that united the solitary—enslaved peons, displaced Indians—against the devourers of lands and their hired guns, and against the World Bank experts who financed the poisoning of the rivers and the razing of the jungle.

Thus he was marked for death.

The gunshots came through the window.

December 16

FIGHT POVERTY: MASSAGE THE NUMBERS

For forty years the mass miscommunications media joyously celebrated steady victories in the war on poverty. Year after year, poverty was beating a hasty retreat.

So it went until today in the year 2007, when experts from the World Bank, with the assistance of the International Monetary Fund and a few United Nations agencies, updated their statistical tables on the world's buying power. In a report by the International Comparison Program, which obtained little or no media coverage, the experts corrected some of the data from earlier measurements. Among other small errors, they discovered that the number of poor people was five hundred million more than previously recorded.

They, the poor, already knew.

December 17

THE LITTLE FLAME

On this morning in 2010, as on every other morning, Mohamed Bouazizi was hauling his cart filled with fruit and vegetables somewhere in Tunis.

As on every other morning, the police arrived to collect the levy they had concocted.

But this morning, Mohamed refused to pay.

The policemen beat him, overturned his cart and stomped all over his fruit and vegetables splattered on the ground.

Mohamed then doused himself from head to foot with gasoline and set himself on fire.

In a few days, that little flame, no taller than a street vendor, grew to encompass the entire Arab world, ablaze with people tired of being nobody.

December 18

The First Exiles

Today, International Migrants Day, is not a bad moment to recall that the first ones in human history obliged to emigrate were Adam and Eve.

According to the official version, Eve tempted Adam: she offered him the forbidden fruit and it was her fault that both of them were banished from Paradise.

But is that how it happened? Or did Adam do what he did of his own accord?

Maybe Eve offered him nothing and asked nothing of him.

Maybe Adam chose to bite the forbidden fruit when he learned that Eve had already done so.

Maybe she had already lost the privilege of immortality and Adam opted to share her damnation.

So he became mortal. But not alone.

December 19

ANOTHER WOMAN EXILED

At the end of 1919, two hundred and fifty "foreign undesirables" left the port of New York, forbidden ever to return to the United States.

Among those heading off into exile was the "highly dangerous foreigner" Emma Goldman, who had been arrested several times for opposing the draft, for promoting contraceptives, for organizing strikes and for other attacks on national security.

Some of Emma's sayings:

"Prostitution is the greatest triumph of Puritanism."

"Is there anything indeed more terrible, more criminal, than our glorified sacred function of motherhood?"

"Heaven must be an awfully dull place if the poor in spirit live there."

"If voting changed anything, it would be illegal."

"Every society has the criminals it deserves."

"All wars are wars among thieves who are too cowardly to fight, and therefore induce the young manhood of the whole world to do the fighting for them."

December 20

The door was closed:
"Who is it?"
"It's me."
"I don't know you."
And the door remained closed.
The following day:
"Who is it?"
"It's me."
"I don't know who you are."
And the door remained closed.
Then the following day:
"Who is it?"
"It's you."
And the door opened.

—From the Persian poet Farid al-Din Attar,
    born in 1142 in the city of Nishapur

December 21

The Joy of Saying

This day could be any other day.

No days in Enheduanna's life are known.

A few facts are: Enheduanna lived four thousand three hundred years ago in the kingdom where writing was invented, now called Iraq,

and she was the first woman writer, the first woman who signed her words,

also the first woman who wrote laws,

and an astronomer, a sage of the stars,

that she suffered exile,

and in writing she sang to the moon goddess Inanna, her protector, and she celebrated the joy of writing, which is a fiesta:

like giving birth,
creating life,
conceiving the world.

December 22

The Joy of Flying

Some people maintain the Wright brothers invented the airplane around this time in 1903, but others insist it happened a couple of years later and Santos-Dumont was the creator of the first machine worthy of that name.

The only thing absolutely certain is that three hundred and fifty million years earlier, a pair of tiny flaps sprouted from the body of a dragonfly's ancestor, and those flaps became wings that grew longer and longer over the next few million years, urged on by the desire to fly.

Dragonflies were the first to travel by air.

December 23

In 1773 the earth trembled from hunger and over the course of a few days it devoured the city now called Antigua, which for more than two centuries had ruled Guatemala and the entire region of Central America.

In religious festivals Antigua rises from its ruins. Its streets become carpets of flowers patterned as suns and fruits and birds of great plumage. No one can tell whether the feet walking on them are celebrating the coming birth of Jesus or the rebirth of the city.

Local people weave these street gardens—patient hands, petal by petal, leaf by leaf—to make Antigua immortal as long as the fiesta lasts.

December 24

A Miracle!

On Christmas Eve in 1991 the Soviet Union passed away, and in the manger Russian capitalism was born.

The new faith worked a miracle: transfigured apparatchiks turned into businessmen, Communist Party leaders changed religion and became brazen nouveaux riches who put a "for sale" sign on the state and bought everything buyable in their country and the world for the price of bananas.

Not even soccer clubs escaped.

December 25

Jesus could not celebrate his birthday because he had no birthday.

In the year 354 the Christians of Rome decided that he had been born on December 25.

That was the day the pagans of the north of the world celebrated the passing of the longest night of the year and the arrival of the sun god, who came to end the darkness.

The sun god came to Rome from Persia.

He had been called Mitra.

Then he was called Jesus.

December 26

Voyage to the Sea

In times gone by the sons of the sun and the daughters of the moon lived together in the African kingdom of Dahomey.

Together they cuddled and squabbled until the gods separated them and condemned them to live far apart.

Ever since, the sons of the sun are fish in the sea and the daughters of the moon are stars in the night.

Starfish do not fall from the sky: they travel from there. And in the waters they seek out their lost lovers.

December 27

THE TRAVELER

Matsuo Bashō was born to be a samurai, but he renounced war and became a poet. A wandering poet.

A month after his death, back in 1694 more or less, the roads of Japan longed for the footsteps of his straw sandals and the words he left hanging from the roofs of the homes that took him in. Like these:

> *Days and months are travelers of eternity.*
> *Thus pass the years.*
> *Those who navigate the sea or ride horses across*
> *the land are forever traveling, until they succumb*
> *under the weight of time.*
> *Many are the men of old who died along the way.*
> *I have only succumbed to the temptation of clouds,*
> *the vagabonds of the sky.*

December 28

NOSTALGIA FOR THE FUTURE

Oscar Niemeyer began the year 2007 with one hundred years under his belt and eight buildings under construction.

The liveliest of all architects had not tired of transforming, project by project, the skyline of the world.

His aged eyes were not fixed on the high heavens that humiliate us; they gazed freshly, happily at the drifting clouds, his source of inspiration for the next creation.

In the clouds he discovered cathedrals, gardens of incredible flowers, monsters, galloping horses, birds with many wings, exploding seas, flying foam and undulating women who offered themselves in the wind and with the wind flew off.

Every time doctors put him in the hospital, believing his time had arrived, Oscar killed his boredom composing sambas and singing them with the nurses.

And that is how this cloud hunter, this pursuer of fugitive beauty, left his first century of life behind and kept right on going.

December 29

The Road Is Destiny

The drinking was copious when we bid good-bye to the departing year, and I got lost in the streets of Cádiz.

I asked how I could get to the market. An old man peeled his back off the wall and very grudgingly replied, pointing nowhere: "You do whatever the street tells you."

The street told me and I made it home.

A few thousand years before, Noah navigated without compass or sails or even a rudder.

His ark drifted wherever the wind bade him, and he was saved from the flood.

December 30

We Are Made of Music

When I cock my ear
I hear tunes that come from far away,
from the past,
from other times,
from hours that are no longer
and from lives that are no longer.
Perhaps our lives
are made of music.
On the day of resurrection,
my eyes will open again in Seville.

—Boabdil, the last
king of Muslim Spain

December 31

In Rome in the year 208, Quintus Serenus Sammonicus wrote *Liber medecinalis*, a book in which he revealed his discoveries in the arts of healing.

Among other remedies, this physician to two emperors, poet and owner of the best library of his time, proposed an infallible way to avoid tertian fever and keep death at bay: by hanging a word across your chest day and night.

The word was "Abracadabra," which in ancient Hebrew meant and still means, "Give your fire until the last of your days."

Contents

January

February

March

April

May

June

July

August

September

October

November

December

Index of Names